CW00402963

Introduction

All layouts begin with a plan. This might be a carefully draughted scale drawing prepared by hand, a pencil sketch scribbled on the back of an envelope, a print-out from one of the numerous track planning software packages available on computer, or even just an idea locked within the mind's eye of the builder. It may even be a layout derived from a plan published in a book or magazine, or downloaded from the internet.

Some railway modellers can plan layouts almost intuitively, using their knowledge and experience of track configurations and train movements, but for most of us we need a starting point. That starting point will almost always be published plans, for it's only by studying published plans that we can begin to learn of all the intricacies and nuances of railway trackwork, model or otherwise.

For decades modellers found inspiration in the numerous little softback booklets prepared by the erstwhile editor of Railway Modeller from 1951 to 1978 – Cyril Freezer. His imagination, knowledge of railway operating practice, and his draughtsman skills enabled him to draw up hundreds of layout plans suitable for all sorts of locations around the home – he even suggested layout designs that could be built in the lounge, hall or landing: nowhere, it seems, is unsuitable for housing a model railway.

Cyril Freezer's plans and booklets are still very popular today, and although model railway and rolling stock dimensional specifications have changed markedly since his time, the plans are as relevant today as they ever were, if for no other reason than sources of layout ideas and inspiration from which modern-sized layout schemes can be adapted.

With this new book *A Compendium of Track Plans* for layouts to suit all locations, we have built on Freezer's legacy and also taken modern ideas from within the hobby as a whole, and now present this brand new collection of plans, which you can either copy in their entirety, or otherwise use them as a basis for developing your own track plan.

With that in mind, we also include a section at the back of the book devoted to practical planning advice, hints and tips. This explains the fundamentals of layout planning and also describes some techniques you can use to check the viability of your plan before you spend money on baseboards and track.

And as you embark on your exciting new layout building project, remember that railway modelling is a very creative and tactile hobby which is well over 100 years old: that's about as old as public broadcast radio, older than television, and much older than computers and all their derivations!

Railway Modelling has been enjoyed by countless thousands of enthusiasts for a very long time: long may the pleasures and fascination continue.

Steve Flint
Senior Editor
Railway Modeller
July 2021

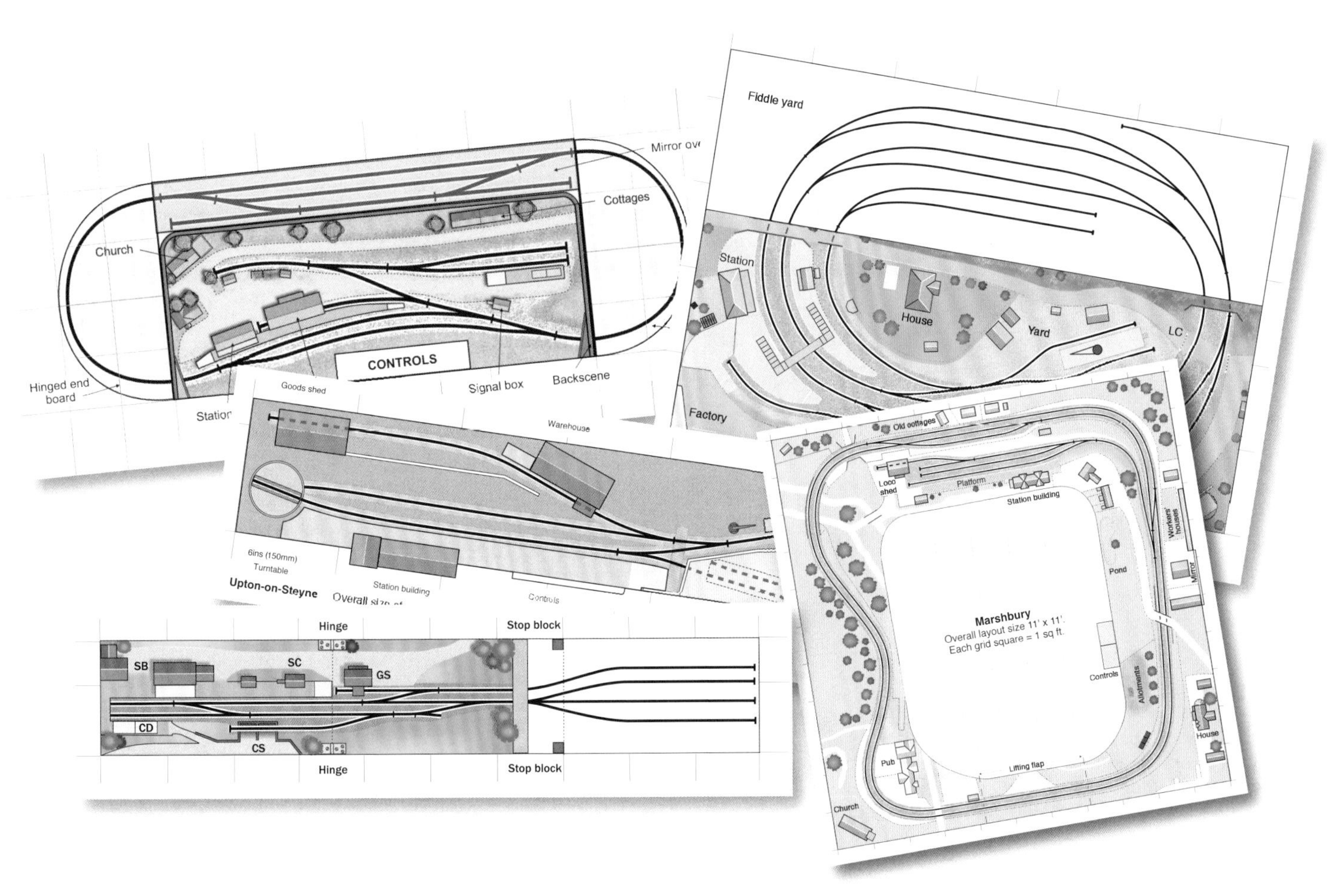

Contents

Scaling the plans for different scales and gauges

All 50 plans in this book are presented with layout sizes shown for OO gauge; e.g. *Overall layout size for OO gauge: 10' x 8'*.

The grid squares equate to 1' x 1' squares for OO gauge; 6" x 6" for N gauge, and 21" x 21" in O gauge.

If scaling any plan for a different gauge, it should be noted that operating areas will be correspondingly reduced or enlarged. Clearances between levels may also be affected and radii of curves may need adjusting. To assist in adapting the plans for different gauges, consult the advice in the final chapter about creating your own plans.

Editor & photographer **Steve Flint**
Art Director **Adrian Stickland**
Production Editor **Tim Rayner**
Graphic Illustration **Brian Meredith, Dave Clements, Gary Bickley**
Chairman **C M Pritchard**

Acknowledgements

This publication would not have been possible without the modelling input of the following, some of whom are sadly no longer with us – John Allison, Don Annison, Simon Atkins, Anthony Bilton, members of Birtley Model Engineers, Ian Blenkinsopp, Trevor Bottomley, Jon Dean, Maurice Deane, Peter Denny, members of the East Yorkshire Finescale Group, Owen Edis, Michael Farr, John Flann, Cyril Freezer, Ian Futers, Ken Gibbons, Simon & Tallon Hamlett, Ken Harland, Graham Jowett-Ive, Dean Knights, Paul Lunn, Ian Macdonald, Paul Marshall-Potter, Paul Mays, Myles Munsey, members of Newport Model Railway Society, Richard Peake, Alan Pike, Mac Pyrke, Stuart Robinson, Neil Rushby, members of the East of Scotland 4mm Group of the Scalefour Society, Stephen Shepherd, Richard Slate, Geoffrey Smith, John Spence, members of the Stafford Railway Circle, Ian Stoate, Jeff Taylor, Gavin Thrum, Adrian Walby, and Martin Wright.

© Peco Publications & Publicity 2021

All rights reserved. No part of this publication may be reproduced or transmitted in any form or by any means, electronic or mechanical, including photocopying, recording or by any information storage and retrieval system, without prior permission in writing from the copyright owners. Multiple copying of the contents of this magazine without prior written approval is not permitted.

That it shall not without the written consent of the publishers be lent, resold, hired out or otherwise disposed of by way of trade at a price in excess of the recommended maximum price or in mutilated condition, or in any unauthorised cover, or affixed to as part of any publication or advertising matter whatsoever.

Views expressed by contributors are not necessarily those of the publishers.

While every care is taken to ensure that the contents of the magazine are correct, the publishers cannot be held responsible for any errors that may occur in the editorial or advertisements nor for the actions of the advertisers..

Printed by
Acanthus Press, 21 Ryelands Business Park
Bagley Road, Wellington, Somerset TA21 9PZ

Peco Publications & Publicity Ltd,
Beer, Seaton, Devon, EX12 3NA, England.
Telephone: 01297 20580 Fax 01297 20229
Website: www.pecopublications.co.uk
Email: railway-modeller@btconnect.com

Chapter 1

Model railway layout formats and design basics

Look at any real railway, be it part of the national rail network, a heritage concern, or even an industrial undertaking, and it is invariably long and thin in its structure and appearance. This means that any replication of a real railway in model form has to be correspondingly long and thin too. Not really an ideal shape for building a miniature version in a spare room, attic or garden shed. But railway modellers are, by their nature, very creative and innovative, and have long found ways in which to bend, curve and squeeze all manner of railway configurations into whatever space they might have at their disposal.

So let us first consider some of the established formats of model railway layouts which you will find as plans in the pages of this book.

The continuous run

Turning the tracks in on themselves and forming a continuous loop has long been the most popular way of creating a model railway layout – indeed every train set ever sold as a Christmas present usually contains a circle of track for starters: and most usually, the next stage on from the train set is to build up a continuous oval of tracks around which your trains can circulate indefinitely.

This perpetual loop of track is known colloquially in the hobby as a 'continuous run' format and many, many layout builders use it as a basis for their own layouts, often dividing it into two specific halves; one half being the scenic section, with all the finely modelled details, landscape and (usually) a 'through' station; the other half being the non-scenic section, which is supposed to represent the 'rest of the railway network' and is known as either the 'fiddle yard' or the 'hidden sidings' where trains can be stopped and started, or continually disassembled and reassembled into different formations by hand.

The advantage of a continuous run format is that trains can be operated to and from the non-scenic section in a prototype manner, as if following a proper timetable, or just simply be left to run continually round and through the scenic section for as long as you wish.

As you will see from the plans in this book, the variations and advantages of the continuous run design are numerous and the reason why so many modellers adopt the format. The train set circuit is a classic example of this format and several are featured in chapter 3. Virtually any size of continuous run can be constructed; the minimum size being dictated by the minimum practical radius of the curved sections of track, whilst the largest size will be constrained only by the depth of your own pocket.

End-to-end

Of course very few real railways operate in circles, they mostly run from point A to point B. London Euston to Glasgow Central, London King's Cross to Edinburgh, London Paddington to Bristol are main line railway examples. All heritage railways do likewise, such as the Keighley & Worth Valley, Severn Valley and the West Somerset railways; they operate from a terminus at one end to a terminus at the other. Prototype railways therefore are regarded as end-to-end railways and this format is also widely used by enthusiasts, be it a terminus to terminus layout; a terminus to fiddle yard layout; or a fiddle yard with through station running to another fiddle yard.

Most often the end-to-end format is the preferred design for enthusiasts with only limited space at their disposal, as will become evident as you study the plans in more detail. Furthermore, end-to-end schemes are the basis of virtually all those minimum space layouts usually described as mini- or micro-layouts. A disadvantage of the end-to-end format is that trains cannot be left to run by themselves, unless some sort of automation or computer control is installed – though for many devotees of automatic train control systems, this increases the fun and enjoyment of building such a railway.

Shunting layouts

Operating a railway layout need not just mean long trains running back and forth, or chasing their tails on continuous loops. An interesting alternative layout, especially suited to those with limited space, is a shunting scheme. Essentially an end-to-end design, freight wagons are swapped back and forth between sidings, or in and out of hidden sections of the layout. There is no opportunity to sit back and just watch the trains run round, but such schemes are often preferred by those enthusiasts who enjoy the building, detailing, painting and weathering of rolling stock and locomotive kits to the highest possible standards, usually making use of true-to-scale three-link type couplings operated by hand.

Shunting layouts need not be confined to just freight workings, they can be embellished with rudimentary branch line type passenger trains, of one or two coaches in length, or just a single passenger railcar. Typically the station facility in this scenario is represented by just half a station platform protruding out from beneath an overbridge which serves as a scenic break.

Although not to every enthusiast's liking, shunting layouts are very popular at exhibitions and shows and many of the smaller plans in this book fall into this category, particularly those in chapter 2 – minimum space plans.

Multi-level layouts

The next trick up the sleeves of railway modellers is the use of multiple levels of trackwork in order to extend the length of run between the various elements of the layout – be it between stations, or between stations and hidden sidings, and so on. We might term multi-level designs as being 'advanced' plans, as there are additional considerations to be taken into account when designing and building such schemes; notably the clearance between different levels and the steepest practical gradients that can be constructed between those levels. All this is explored in chapter 6, and as you will see, multi-level layouts can take many forms and incorporate a complex mix of continuous run and end to end formats in one huge layout. In that sense, a well designed multi-level scheme can provide the best of all worlds; end-to-end operation for authentic timetable running, continuous running when you want to simply watch the trains go by, and sections for shunting activities when you want to indulge in a little bit of quiet contemplation.

Portable and fold-away layouts

If you visit one of the many hundreds of model railway exhibitions up and down the country, and indeed across the world, you will find that all the layouts on display are portable in some way. They are designed to be broken down into smaller units for storage and transportation purposes. A portable layout can take any of the above formats, the only proviso being that the joints between individual boards have to be carefully designed such that they can be joined and taken apart many times and still ensure 100% reliable running when fully assembled. The principles of portable construction can be adopted by enthusiasts who don't have room at home for a permanent layout. We can term such a layout as fold-away, in that it can be erected for working on and running trains, but can be taken down and stored in a cupboard or elsewhere, when the domestic space is needed for other purposes. Garages, guest rooms and studies are the usual temporary homes for fold-aways, but even the main lounge can be utilised if need be.

We have included a few plans of some straightforward fold-away designs in chapter 7. The topic of construction of such layouts is very extensive and beyond the scope of this book, but numerous ideas and examples are frequently found in articles in Railway Modeller.

Fiddle yards

As briefly mentioned above, the term 'fiddle yard' has been part of model railway vernacular for decades. No one, it seems, knows how the name originated, but all enthusiasts know what one is: a section of the layout that is off-stage, usually non-scenic, to and from which trains are operated as if travelling to the rest of the railway network. Once safely in the fiddle yard trains can be swapped, turned around and re-marshalled by hand before being sent back out into the layout proper. In other words we are fiddling the fact that the trains don't actually go anywhere once they enter the off-stage section – hence 'fiddle yard' an appropriate enough description for a railway yard in which a lot of fiddling is performed!

It will come as no surprise then, that fiddle yards come in various shapes, sizes and configurations: there are ladder yards, traversers, sector plates, out-and-back loops, cassette systems and so on. A confusing array for the newcomer to model railways, and as many of the plans in this book are illustrated without their associated fiddle yard sections (for reasons of space) we have included a special section on fiddle yards in chapter 8 under the title of Off-stage layout sections.

Layout wiring

It was common practice years ago to show the positions of track power feeds, isolating tracks and insulated rail breaks in model railway plans. Since the advent of Digital Command Control, as opposed to analogue track sectional control, and the optional use of insulated or live frog pointwork, deriving a universally appropriate wiring scheme for model railway plans is now impractical. Furthermore, there are many ways in which layouts can be wired and different enthusiasts prefer different solutions. Accordingly we recommend that once you have decided on your track plan, you should undertake further research to establish the optimum method of wiring the track to suit your choice of control system and points.

Other titles which cover this topic in great depth are available from Peco Publications and can be found in the suggested further reading panel (below) or by visiting the Peco Publications website – **www.pecopublications.co.uk**

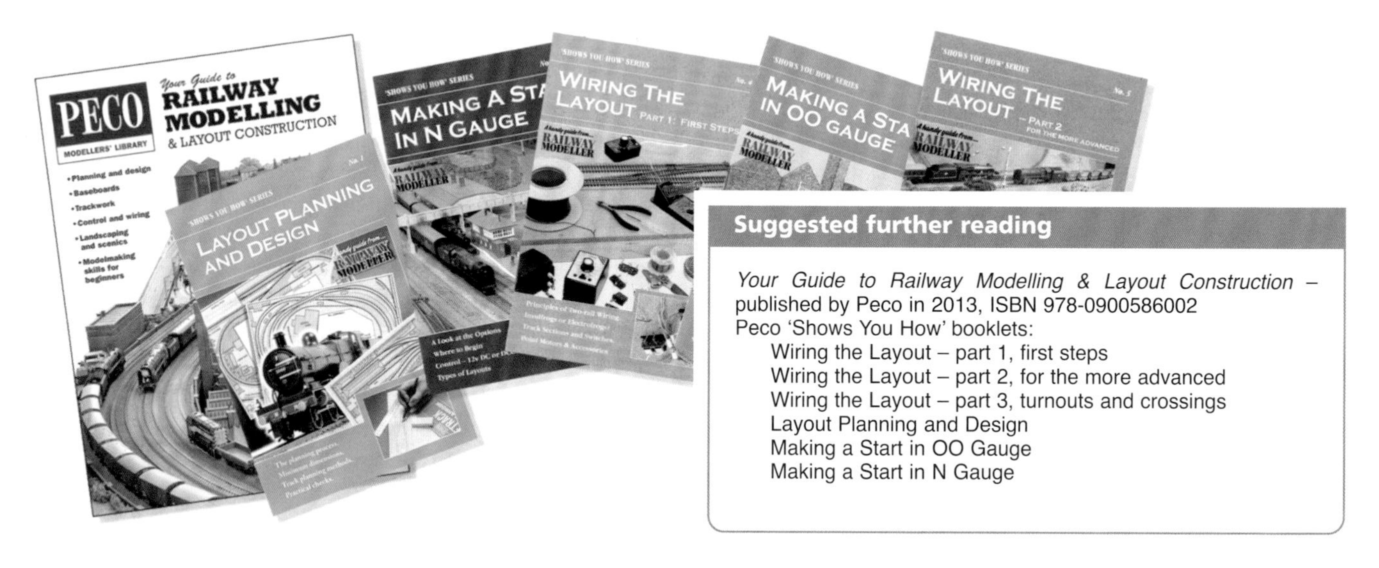

Suggested further reading

Your Guide to Railway Modelling & Layout Construction – published by Peco in 2013, ISBN 978-0900586002
Peco 'Shows You How' booklets:
- Wiring the Layout – part 1, first steps
- Wiring the Layout – part 2, for the more advanced
- Wiring the Layout – part 3, turnouts and crossings
- Layout Planning and Design
- Making a Start in OO Gauge
- Making a Start in N Gauge

Chapter 2

Minimum space plans

Often referred to as mini- or micro-layouts, these ultra compact schemes make ideal small projects for modellers wanting to build something in the tiniest of spaces, or alternatively as a pilot scheme, to try out some new techniques or accessories. Inevitably having only very short runs of track, these layouts are of the end-to-end style and thus operating potential is limited to shunting manoeuvres. That said, another positive benefit of these schemes is that they are relatively inexpensive to build and can be finished quickly. So whilst not everybody's idea of a dream layout, they can each be fulfilling in their own right, and many enthusiasts use the concept time after time, building dozens of layouts in the course of their model making lives. One such enthusiast well known in the *genre* is Ian Futers, and it is with two of his own schemes that we begin this chapter.

Plan No.1

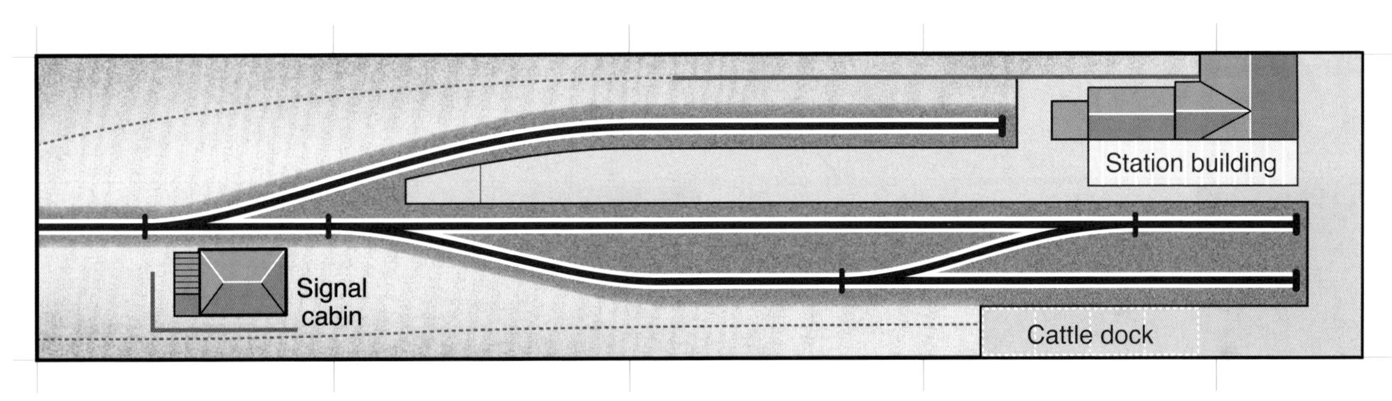

Ashleigh Overall size of scenic section in OO: 4' 6" x 1'

Plan No.2

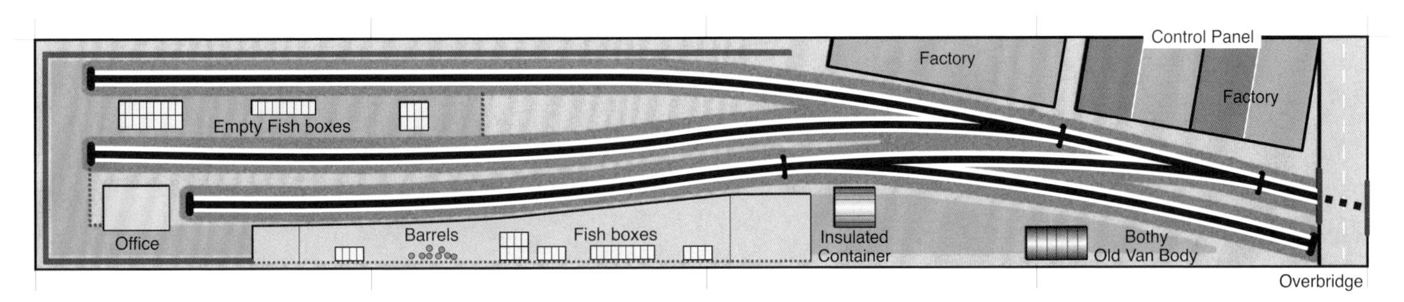

Fisherrow Yard Overall size of scenic section (for OO gauge version): 4' x 8"

Ashleigh and Fisherrow

Ashleigh was Ian's first published layout in September 1972. It represented a north country branch terminus which contains about the barest minimum of steam age railway facilities; a rural station building, signal box, cattle dock and bay platform for goods activities. Some 40 years later he built *Fisherrow Yard*, this time in O gauge and to his now legendary three-point plan format. He deliberately avoided including a run round loop so that it would be necessary to use two locomotives for shunting purposes.

Coupled to a small sector plate type fiddle yard, either plan makes for a compact layout suitable for any scale. Choosing between the two offers a choice between operating passenger and goods services, or just freight only.

The overall station roof

Some railway companies gave their branch line termini short overall roofs to protect the passengers from the vagaries of the British weather. The most well known of these small roof structures is probably those of the Great Western Railway, such as those at the former stations of Moretonhampstead and Ashburton. Other companies such as the Highland and Great North of Scotland railways used this short overall roof concept at a number of localities too, as these two plans suggest; plan 3 being originally designed by Ken Gibbons as a might-have-been terminus at Port Pennan, and plan 4 by Adrian Walby, portraying a fictitious HR station at Lochinver. It should be noted that numerous other railways also used similar designs such as for example; the Furness (Coniston), Great Eastern (at Cromer) and North Eastern (at Richmond), demonstrating that the format is appropriate for many alternative locations. Of course, considerable compression in length must be employed in all cases.

Plan No.3

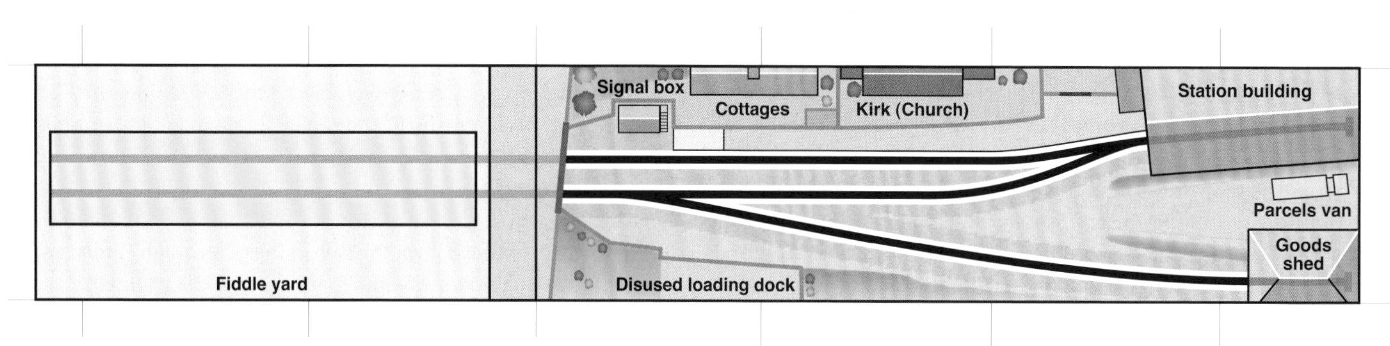

Port Pennan Overall size of scenic section in OO: 3' 7" x 1'.

Plan No.4

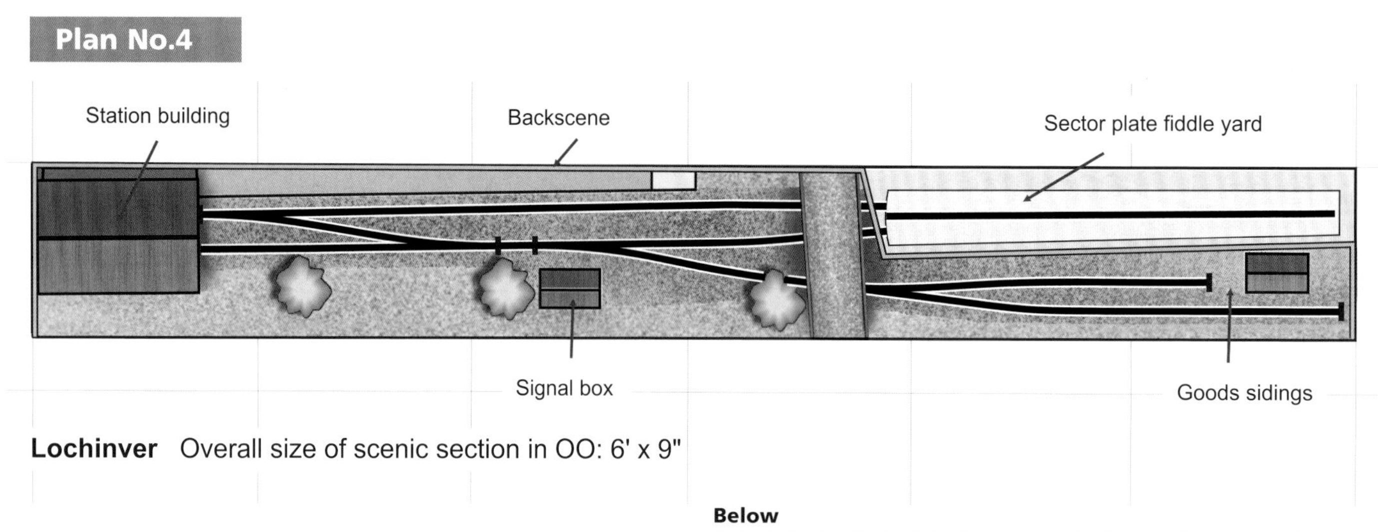

Lochinver Overall size of scenic section in OO: 6' x 9"

Below
Trains in the Far North of Scotland were typically quite short, so a project based on the region will make a good micro-layout.

Small turntables

Withernsea station in East Yorkshire and Bembridge on the Isle of Wight had small turntables at the end of the station platform.

These were just long enough to accommodate a short locomotive and alleviated the need for a separate headshunt and pointwork for a run round loop. The format is not widely used in model form, perhaps because it was not that widely used in the real world, but prototypes do exist, as those two examples mentioned above. Plan 5 is based on *Upton-on-Steyne*, a layout designed and built by the late John Allison, it was a favourite format of his and he actually rebuilt the layout several times in the course of his life. *Upton-on-Steyne* is shown right, the turntable is just out of shot at the bottom left of the picture.

Plan 6 is based on a design idea hatched by Paul Mays as a representation of the aforementioned Bembridge terminus on the Isle of Wight. The backscene is curved at the ends to eliminate those awkward square corners that occur in backscenes when they are built around the baseboard perimeter.

Although based on an Isle of Wight station, anyone interested in this plan format could well develop it for any period and locality in the steam age.

Right
The late John Allison was a staunch supporter of British HO for many years – as with the version of *Upton-on-Steyne* pictured here – and also of economical use of modelling materials.

Plan No.5

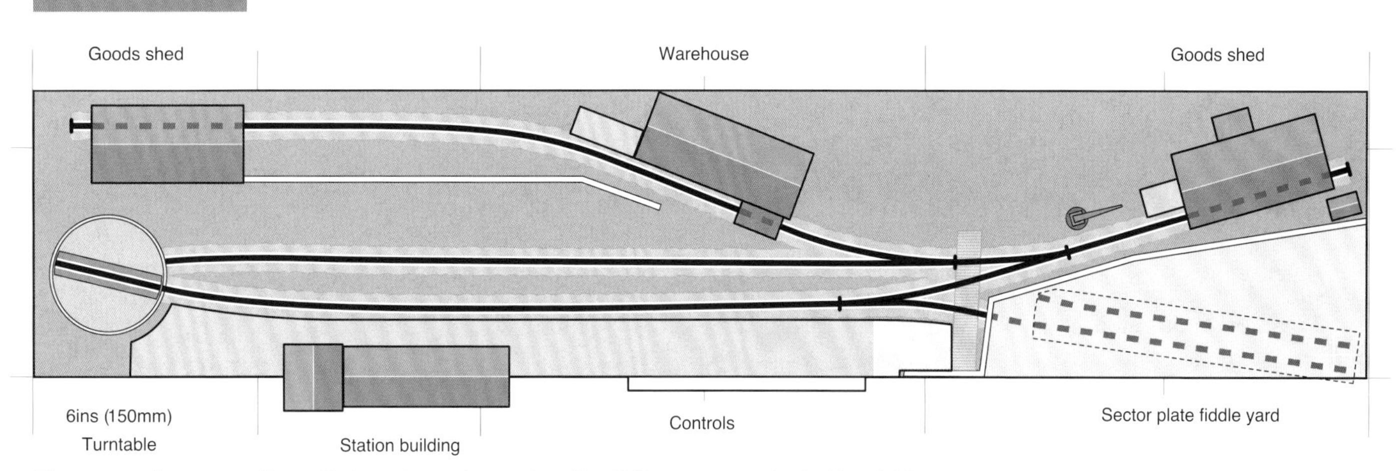

Upton-on-Steyne Overall size of scenic section (for OO gauge version): 6' x 1' 3"

Plan No.6

Overall size of layout in OO gauge: 7' x 1' 3"

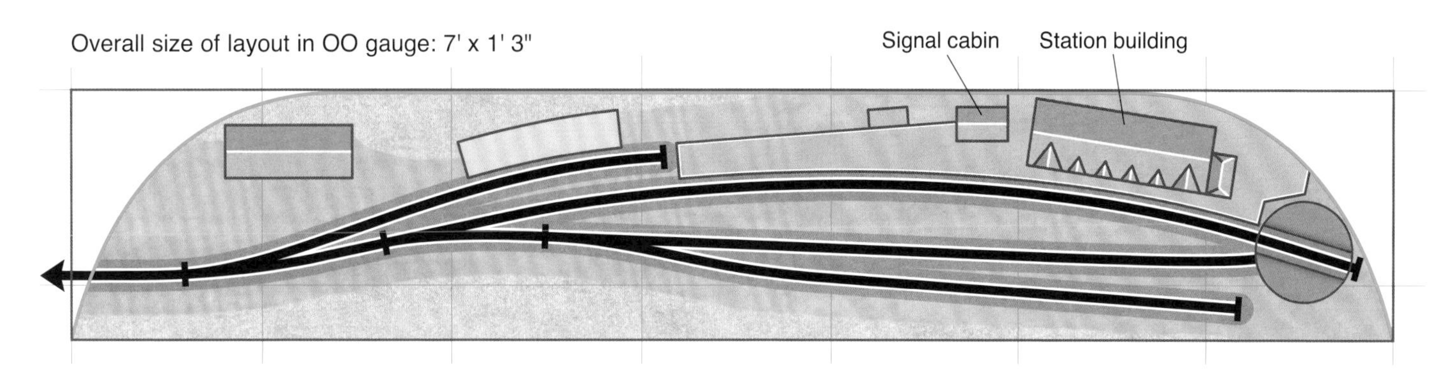

Adapting the prototype

Here we have two plans derived from actual prototype stations, both diminutive branch line halts. One is Smallford, in Hertfordshire (plan 7), built for the former Hatfield & St Albans Railway, as suggested by Paul Marshall-Potter, and the other serving the village of Settrington, in East Yorkshire, on the former Driffield to Malton Railway (later NER and LNER). Being through stations, they need fiddle yards, or at least 'fiddle sidings', at each end, and thus perhaps mean that the schemes are not quite so minimum space as they seem at first. However the scenic section could be built as a stand-alone unit, suited to those who enjoy modelling more than operating, adding the fiddle yard boards for full operating sessions when the desire bites. Both plans are quite similar in configuration, the sidings being shunted in one direction only as was often the case with steam age branch lines, and readily adaptable to your chosen railway company.

Right
Ex-GNR 0-6-0T No 1247 as restored to original condition, is seen passing through Smallford hauling a special train of brake vans packed with eager enthusiasts on 17 June 1961. ***Photograph by Philip J Kelley***

Plan No.7

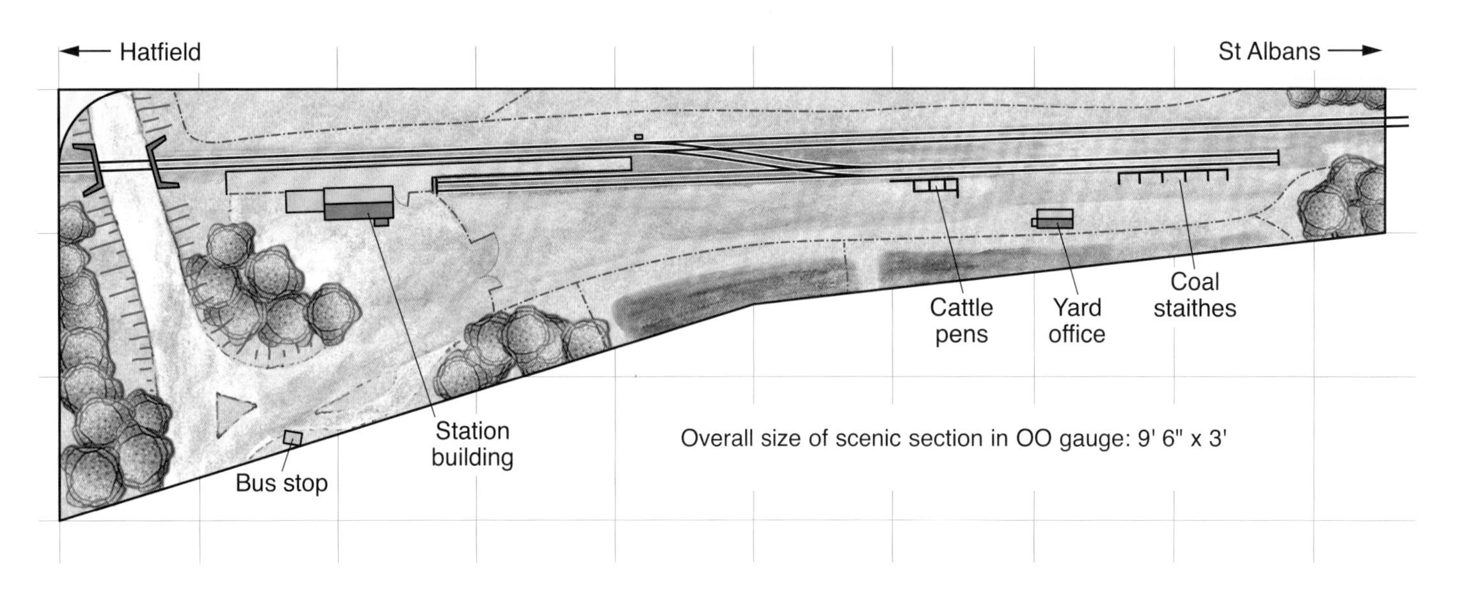

Plan No.8

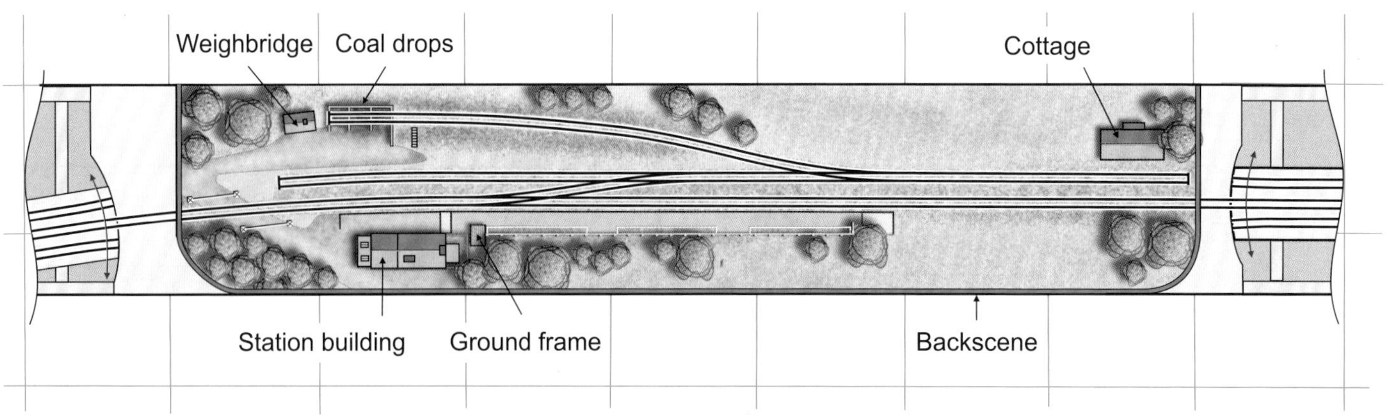

Overall size of scenic section in OO: 7' x 1' 4"

Plan No.9

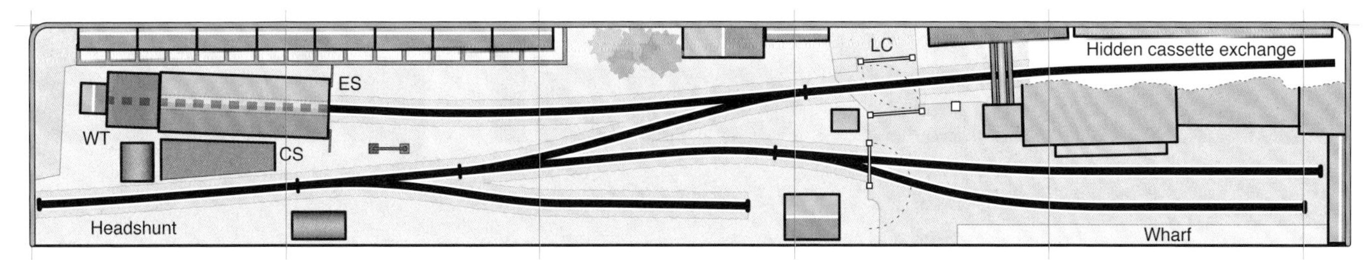

Overall size of layout in OO gauge: 5' x 11"

Freight only

We finish this section with two plans for freight only operating, again designed for the steam age enthusiast, though early diesel shunters could easily be used instead of the inevitable steam 'Pugs'.

Plan 9 is based on the *Castle Wharf Yard* scheme built by Richard Peake. Essentially a quayside scene with additional warehousing, he incorporated a Peco loco lift as a detachable fiddle yard. Although only long enough for a shunter and a couple of wagons, it was sufficient for the job in hand.

Plan 10 follows a design by Neil Rushby, which imagines a small rail yard serving a factory site, which could be anything from steel foundry to a furniture manufacturer. The line along the back of the layout is supposedly the branch line so some short passenger services could be added, running back and forth between the two hidden siding sections.

Right
A freight only layout means that a convincing train need only be three or four wagons long, rather than three or four coaches, so the space taken up by the train is much reduced.

Plan No.10

Overall size of layout in OO gauge: 6' x 1' 8"

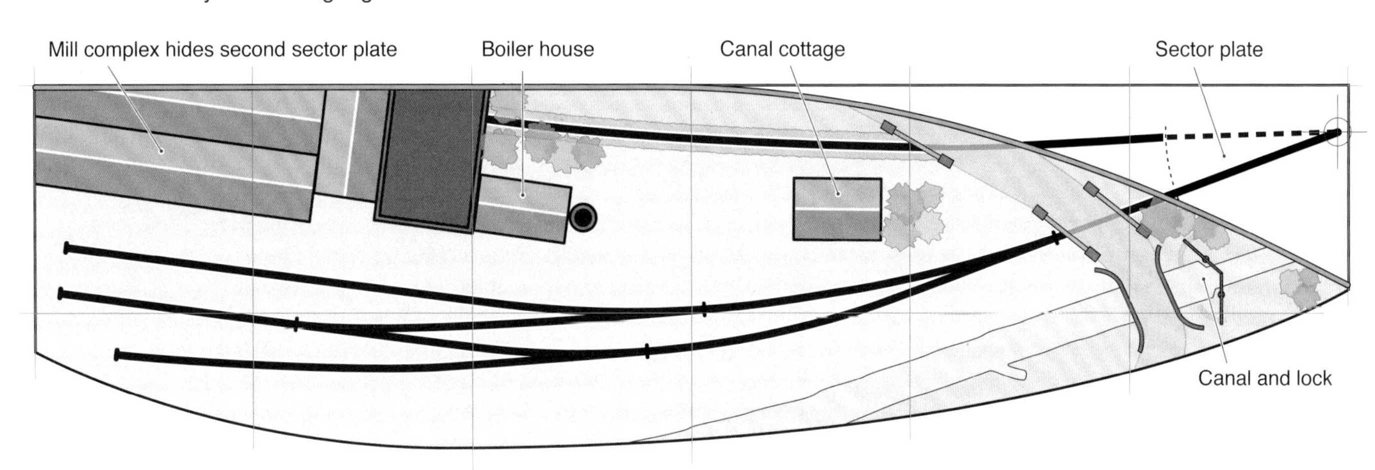

Chapter 3

Classic oval plans

Ever since the introduction of the 'train set' as a Christmas or birthday present, the oval of track on a solid-top board has been the essential caricature of what model railway layouts are all about. Of course there is much more to the hobby, but it is worth pondering a moment on the fact that the oval table top layout served as a first introduction to model railways for many, many enthusiasts. In this chapter we look at some of the many ways the classic oval can be expanded into a true model railway, still within modest proportions, and what better to start than with a plan derived from an original design by the man who became the doyen of the classic oval layout, former editor of RAILWAY MODELLER C J Freezer.

Plan No.11

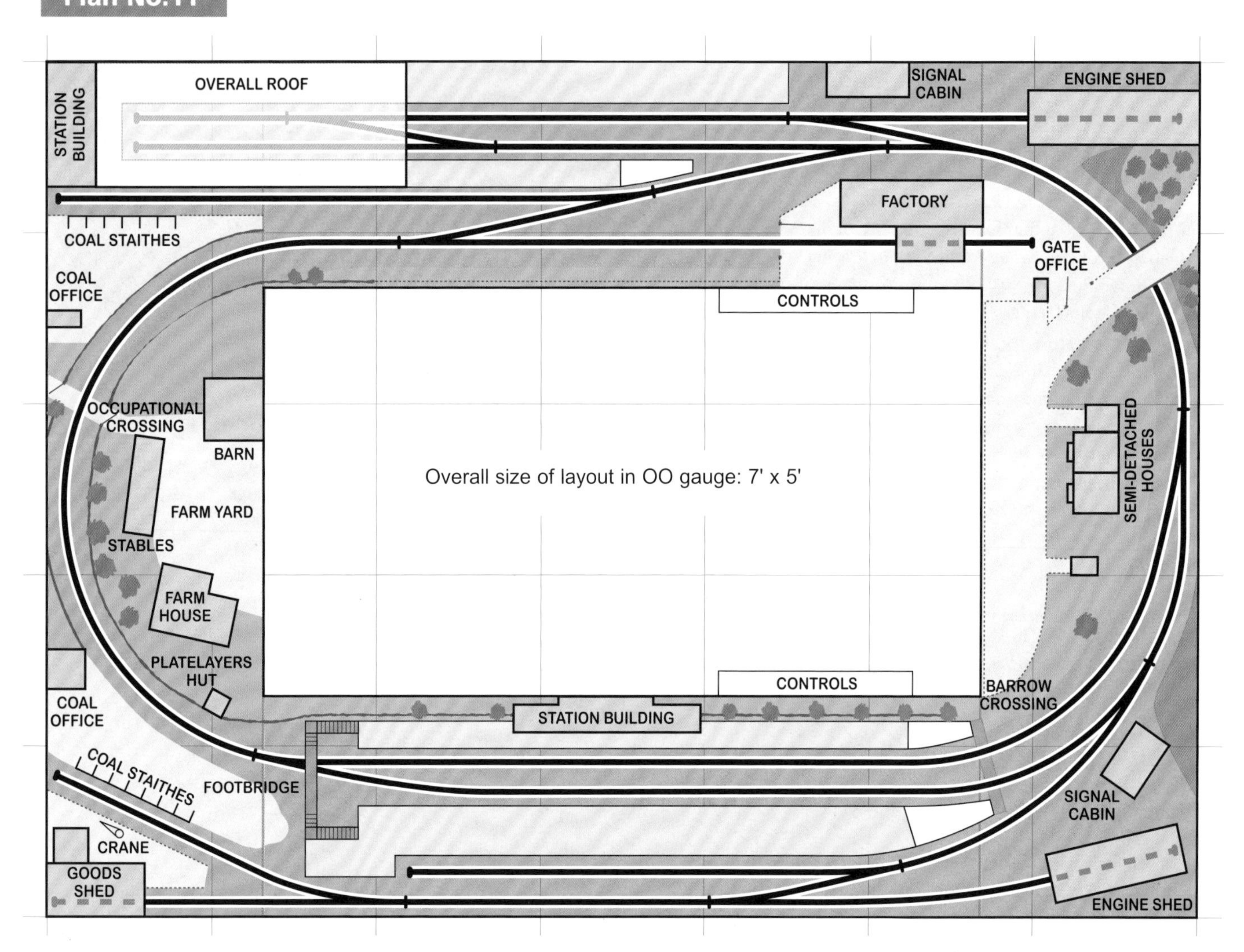

A Freezer classic

The classic oval layout does not need to be built onto a solid top board, in fact it can be more versatile if it is constructed with a central operating area as shown in this updated version of one of C J Freezer's original plans.

Occupying an area of 8' x 5' in OO gauge, it can be housed comfortably at one end of a spare room or within a garden shed or other outhouse. Trains can be operated either as end-to-end or be left to circulate the continuous run section for as long as one might wish. There is no provision for a fiddle yard, but as the operator sits in the middle of the activity, he or she cannot see the whole layout at any one time, thus giving the illusion that trains actually travel somewhere. Though, as with all the plans in this book with central operating areas, if scaling down for use with N gauge equipment, the central area will be too small to use as an operating space and should therefore be filled in with more scenery.

Plan No.12

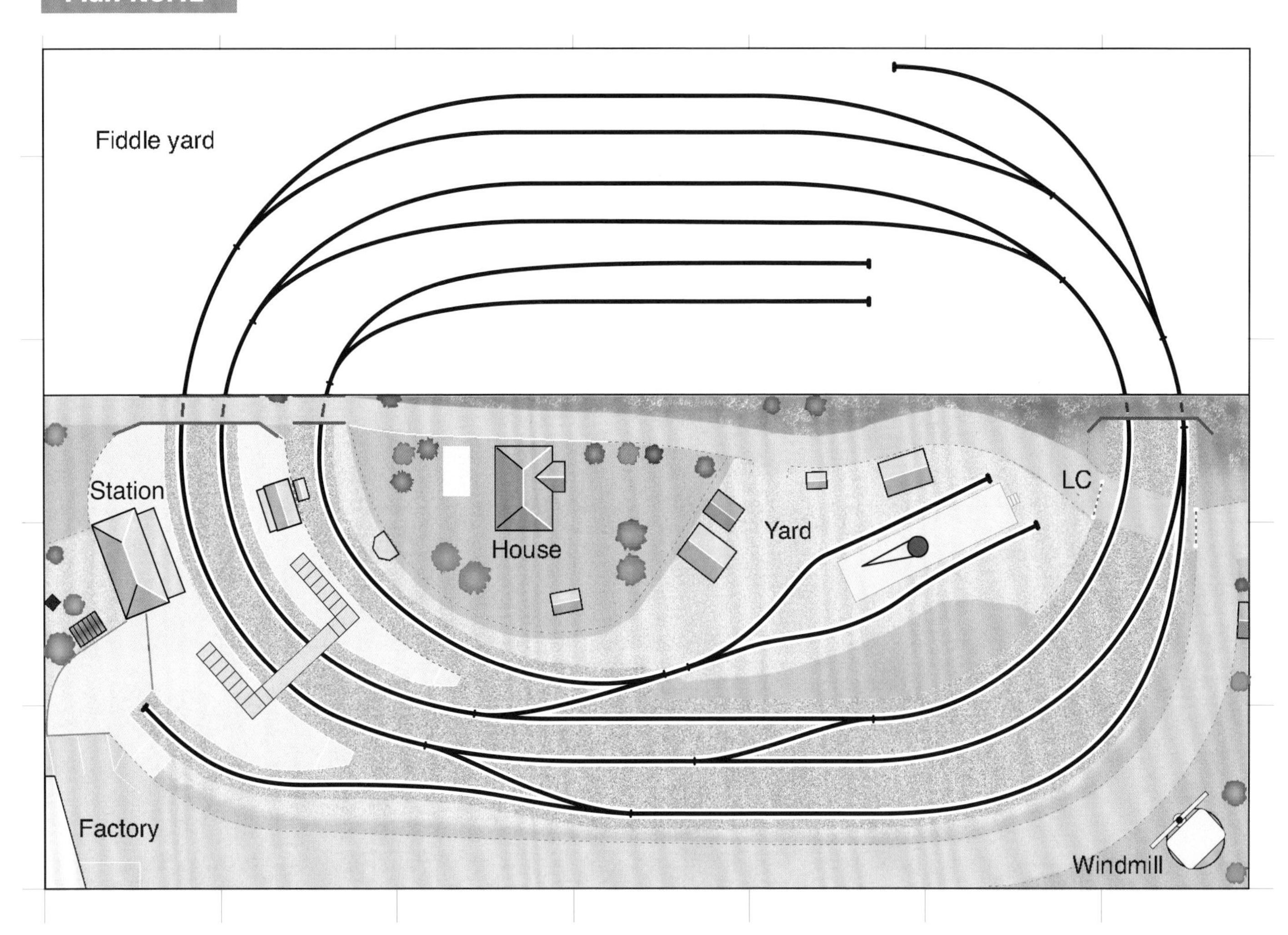

Overall size of layout in OO gauge: 7' x 5'

Half and Half

This oval plan was designed by Simon and Tallon Hamlett and was built onto a solid-top board. It conveniently divides the continuous run into a scenic section and a non-scenic section or fiddle yard. It is actually a double track loop so two trains can operate in opposite directions simultaneously: there is a third section on which shunting operations can be carried out in the yard. There is also provision for a further train to be held in the loop at the front of the layout. This is a scheme which would benefit from the use of DCC control, as in fact was used by the father and son team who built it. At 6'10" x 4'7" in OO gauge, the solid-top board is quite a hefty structure to move around if required, but with a few adjustments to the track configuration the board could be constructed in two more manageable halves.

Right
A Class 25 hauled train of coal wagons on *Tallonstown*, the celebration of the 'traditional' 6' x 4' or thereabouts solid-top baseboard, updated with modern refinements such as digital command control.

Soulby – the Settle & Carlisle in a nutshell

Based on a design by Alan Pike, this plan provides for a double track main line through station, which could technically be anywhere in the country if desired, but takes a likeness to that found at wayside stations on the famous Settle to Carlisle route through the Pennines. At just 10' x 5' in OO gauge it is very compact for this scale, but perfectly possible to build (the pointwork has been sized for Peco Streamline curved, small and medium turnout components), it is not possible to include pointwork for conventional fiddle yard loops, so a small traverser has been designed into the space, (see chapter 8). Although only suitable for short trains of about four coaches/12 wagons in length, it does demonstrate that a main line continuous run can be built in a compact space.

Plan No.13

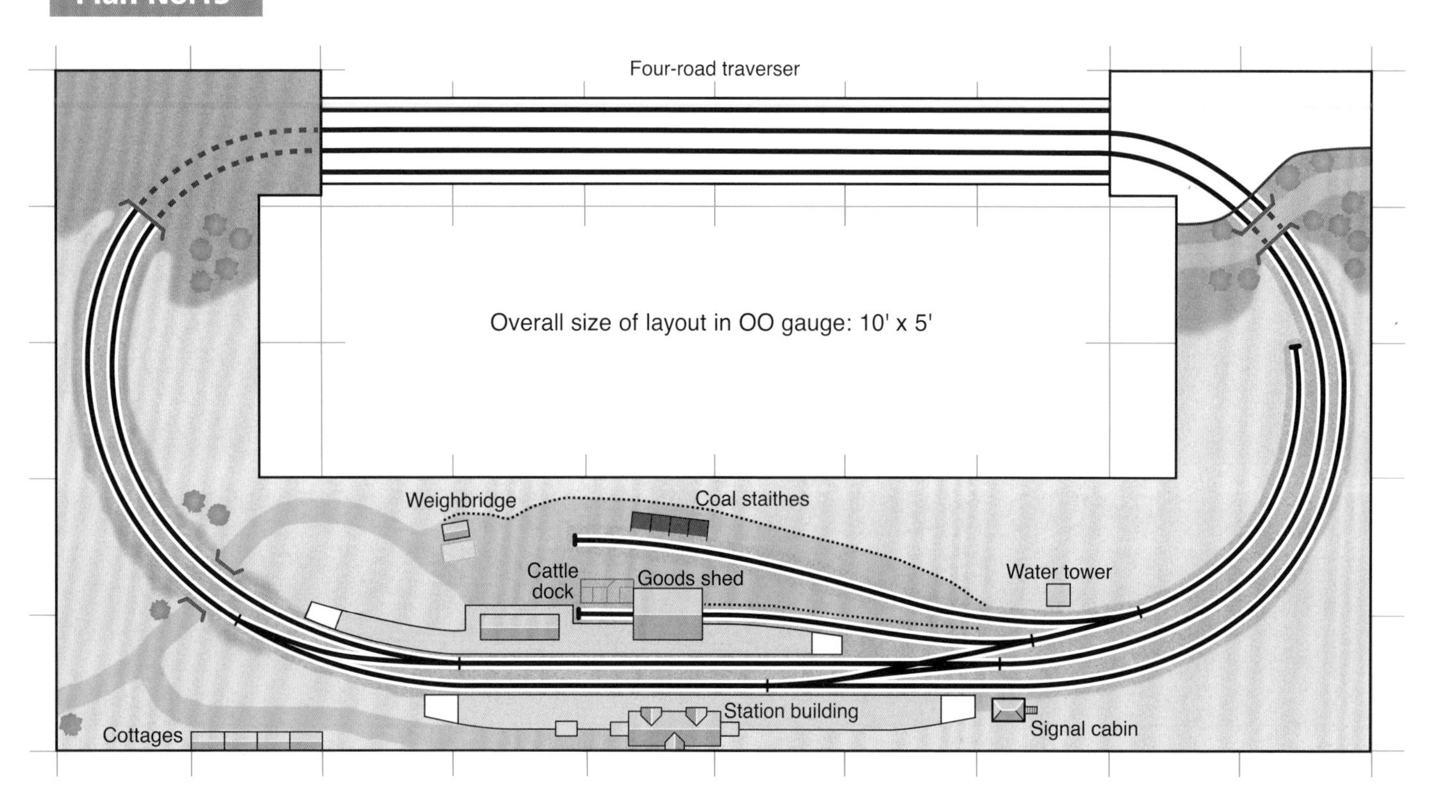

Above
Essence of the Settle & Carlisle, on *Kirkby Stephen West* by Ian Macdonald and Martin Wright; Patriot 4-6-0 No.45518 *Bradshaw* passes the 'typically S&C' station building.

Plan No.14

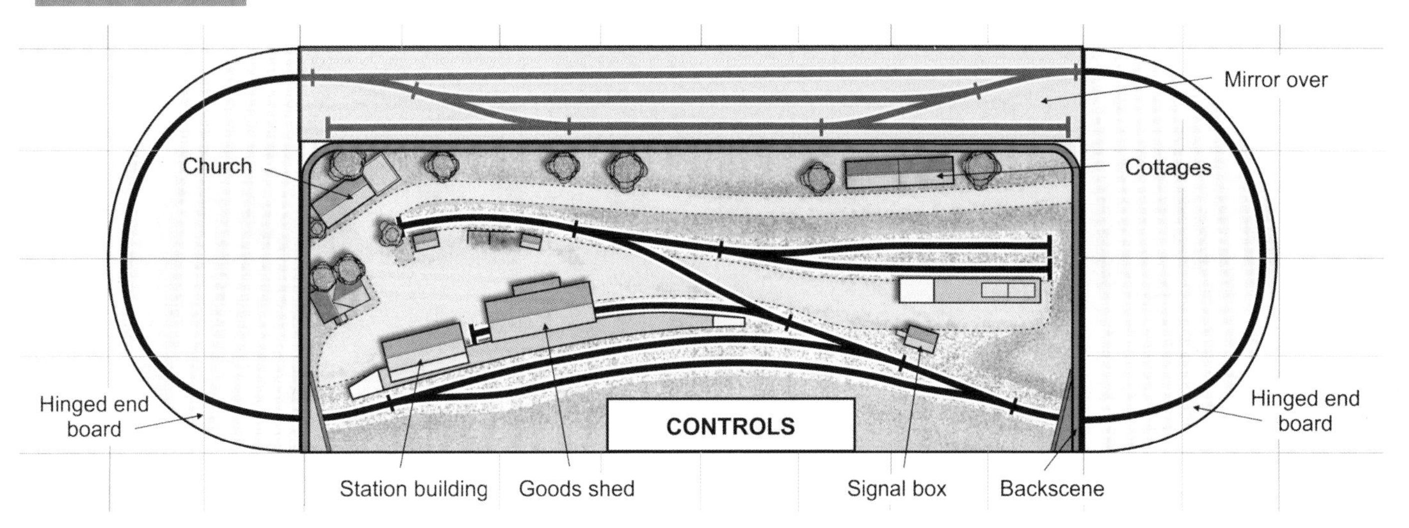

Overall size of layout in OO gauge: 12' x 4'

Day return to Ashcombe

Originally designed for N gauge and built and exhibited by John Spence, this take on the classic oval used fold-down boards for the curves at either end. This assisted with the transportation of the layout which was built for exhibition purposes. This folding idea could be copied, or the curves built as permanent ones and scenery added if preferred. Although built to depict a bucolic GWR country branch line station the plan is readily adaptable to any company or region as befits the builder's interests.

Below
What could shout 'GWR branch line train' better than a Pannier tank and a B set? The archetypal combination is seen in model form running into Ashcombe station on John Spence's N gauge version of the plan.

Plan No.15

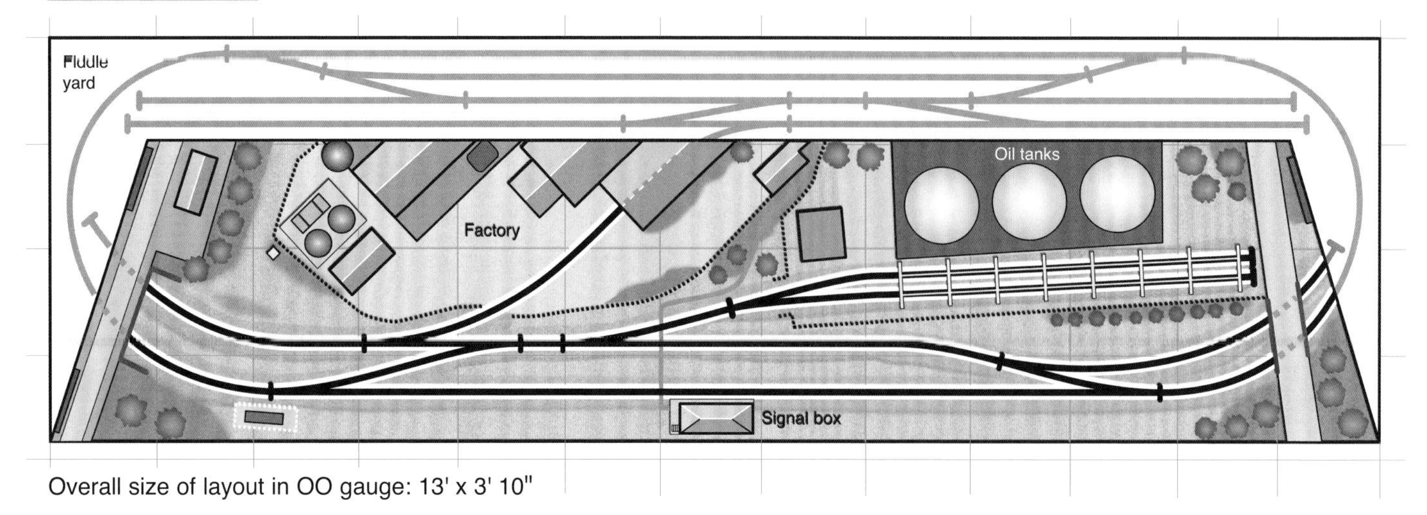

Overall size of layout in OO gauge: 13' x 3' 10"

Industrial or rural?

These two plans were originally designed and built in N gauge, to which both are particularly suited, although both could be scaled up to either OO, as shown, or even O gauge. Plan 15 incorporates an oil storage terminal with two sidings for holding oil or petrol tankers, it was designed and built as *Lofthole* by Jon Dean. The rural plan, Plan 16, takes us all the way to Cumbria for a rendition of the old Cockermouth, Keswick & Penrith Railway route through northern Lakeland and along the banks of Bassenthwaite. This plan and the model is the work of Don Annison.

Below
A large industry need not take up much space in N, as demonstrated by Jon Dean's oil terminal. ***Photograph by Ian Manderson***

Plan No.16

Rock cutting
SB
Level crossing
SC
Optional fiddle yard
Lake
SC

Overall size of layout in OO gauge: 13' x 5'

Below
The beauty of Lakeland in miniature, as a 4F saunters alongside the waters of Bassenthwaite Lake with a freight train on Don Annison's N gauge version.

Poppy Hollow to Barley Dean

Your author has a little confession to make, as this plan, derived from a two station layout built by John Flann in the late 1960s, was one of those layouts which helped to seal my lifelong interest in the hobby. Fondly remembered in the pages of *Model Railway News* from that time, when my predecessor here at RAILWAY MODELLER, John Brewer, was the then editor. Basically it is a simple and conventional oval plan featuring a pair of dis-similar branch passing stations, and modelled (inevitably) in the Great Western branch line idiom. It has a central operating area, again to create the perception that trains actually go somewhere, and it can be readily used for other companies and regions as the fancy takes. If scaled down to N, the central area would be just too small to accommodate a scale human operator, so it would be better on this occasion to upsize the footprint a little, and include longer runs and shallower radius curves. Nevertheless a straightforward but interesting and attractive plan for any scale.

Above
A Dean Goods arrives at Barley Dean with a milk train, on the early incarnation of John Flann's Great Western empire, as published in a 1960s edition of *Model Railway News. Photograph by Roy Dock*

Plan No.17

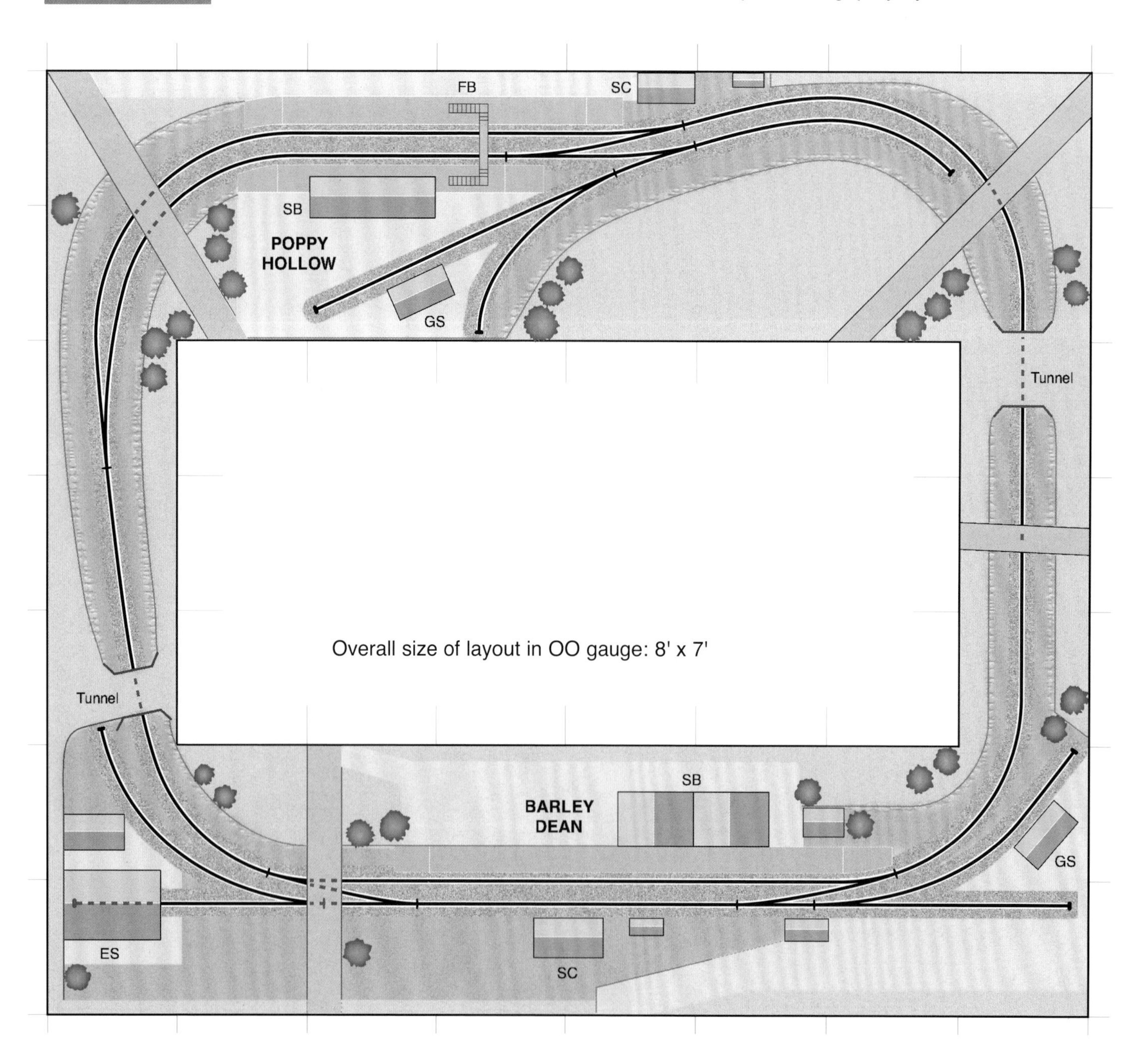

Plan No.18

Marshbury

This plan by Geoffrey Smith is a spacious double track continuous run with plenty of scope for rural – or if you prefer – urban scenery. Although Geoffrey's version occupies a brick shed, any room 11' x 11' would be suitable. The track design is that which would now be found on the modern railway, as seen in the accompanying photograph, with a loop for holding a freight train which is accessible to/from both main lines.

The main line, which is at a slightly higher level than the terminus station, and allows trains to be seen running through the scenery. The lower level station is intended as a heritage railway site to enable a few preserved steam locomotives to be operated as well as typical modern main line diesel locomotives.

The plan could easily be adapted to include lots more track and sidings if desired, but the essence of *Marshbury* is to be able to sit back, relax and watch the trains go by.

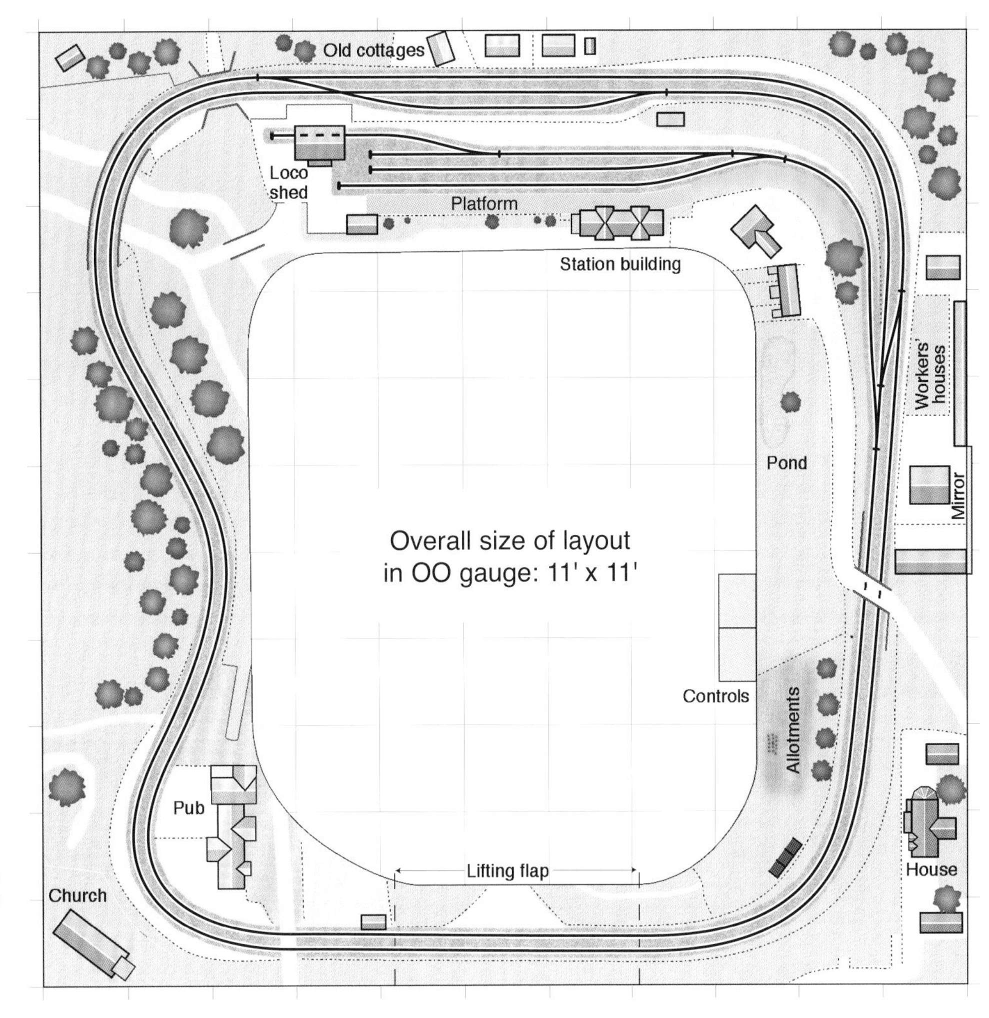

Chapter 4

End-to-end plans

End-to-end layouts are universally popular in that they can be built in long-thin formats along one wall or around the perimeter walls of a spare room. As previously mentioned trains cannot be left to run indefinitely, but must be operated in a railwaylike manner from the outset, which is often the appeal of the format. Moreover, if you want to make an accurate model of a real station, the end to end format is usually ideal. One golden rule I adopt when considering an end-to-end design is that the minimum total length of the layout including fiddle yards needs to be at least three times the length of the longest train you wish to run. That is, one third of the layout length for it to start from, one third of the length whilst moving, and the third and final length for the train to end its journey. Thus a train 3' (1m) in length needs a layout at least 9' (3m) from one end to the other – not always necessary but a useful yardstick when considering end-to-end layout formations.

Once again let's start this chapter with another updated version of C J Freezer's most widely known end-to-end plan: *Minories*, a suburban-style station terminus. A second enlarged version of the plan which features a goods warehouse is also included.

Plan No.19

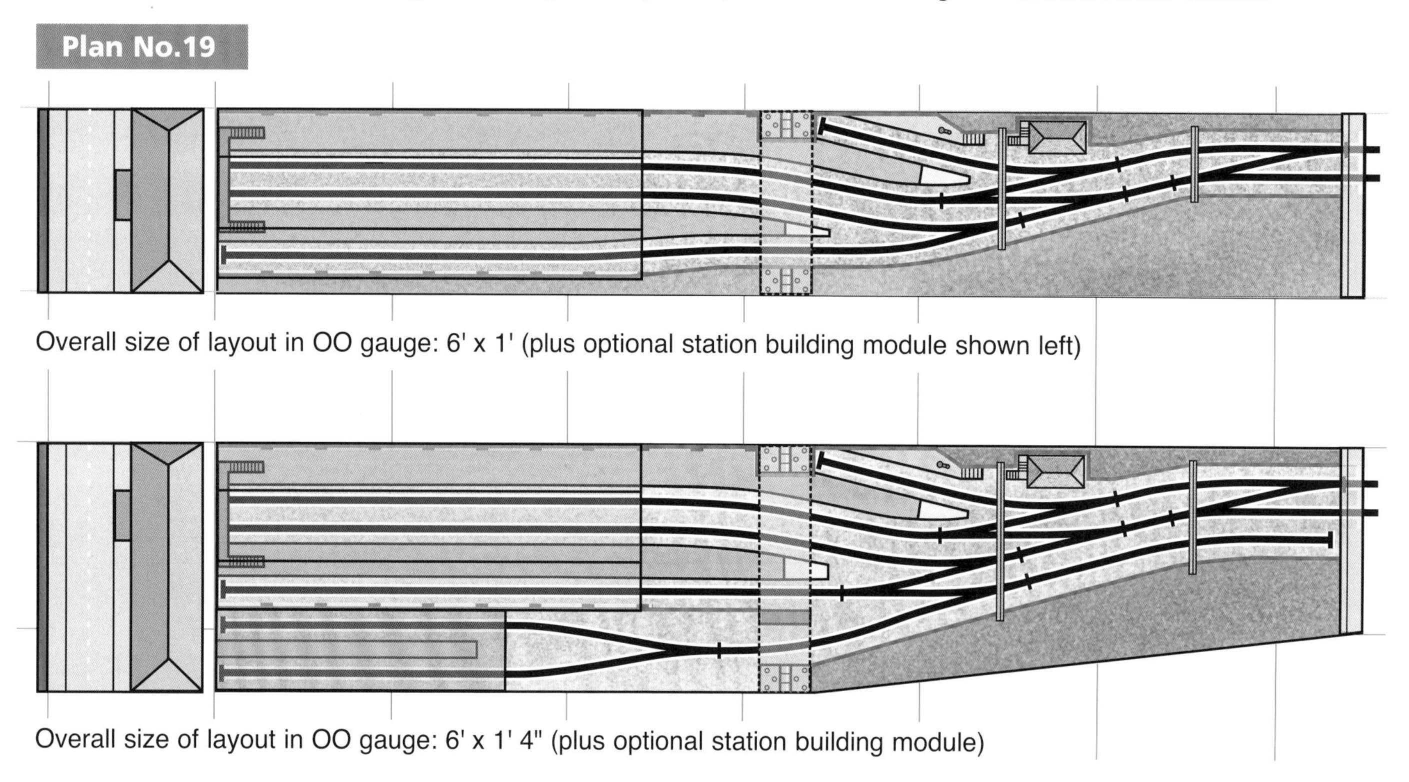

Overall size of layout in OO gauge: 6' x 1' (plus optional station building module shown left)

Overall size of layout in OO gauge: 6' x 1' 4" (plus optional station building module)

Minories

Originally published in 1957, this abiding plan is just as relevant today as it was then. Designed with suburban steam trains in mind and operated on a top and tail basis, today it would probably only see a stream of multiple unit types coming and going. (Top and tail operations means that when a steam locomotive-hauled train arrives in the terminus, a fresh loco is attached to the last coach to form an outbound train which, once it departs, leaves the original loco standing at the buffers. This then proceeds to the stabling point to await the next arrival.) In his original scheme, Freezer saw this plan as a potential foldaway layout and included backflap hinges in the plan cunningly disguised by a removable road overbridge. This would of course be optional.

Left
The spirit of *Minories* updated with *Somers Town* by Jeff Taylor, which was an entry in a DEMU competition in 2007 to celebrate the 50th anniversary of this popular design.

Plan No.20

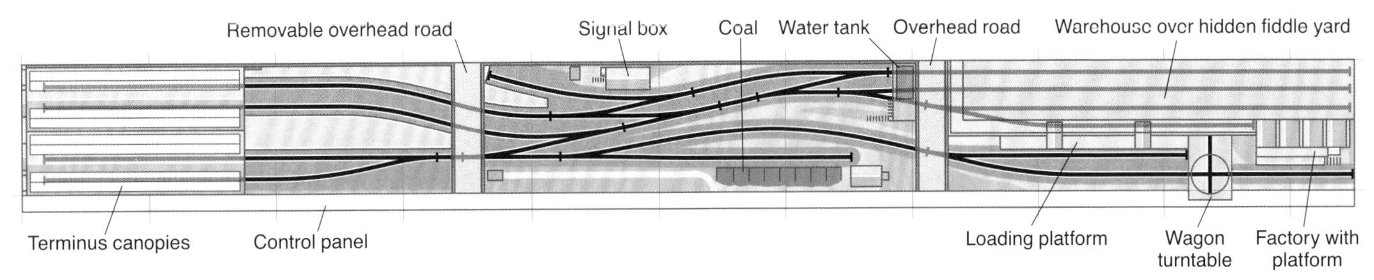

Overall size of layout in OO gauge: 10' 6" x 13½"

Great Moor Street

Minories provides a basic plan that is ripe for adaptation or development into a larger passenger terminus plan; and here is one such example built by Gavin Thrum who lives in Australia. Gavin's plan includes a fiddle yard which is hidden behind a row of Metcalfe Models' low-relief warehouses assembled so as to create an old style steam age goods warehouse. At just 10'6" long at 13½" wide the plan packs an awful lot of railway into its small footprint and is capable of accommodating trains up to a length equivalent to three BR standard Mk.I coaches, or four suburban length vehicles.

Equally, the plan can be adjusted for depicting the modern era, with the goods warehouse being converted into an apartment building and, perhaps, a steam railway preservation society occupying the old sidings – possibly even running heritage services to and from the front platform face.

Below
A quiet moment between trains on *Great Moor Street*, which evokes the atmosphere of the former LNWR. *Photograph by Gavin Thrum*

Along the garage wall

The average garage can be up to 18' long and space can often be found along one of the side walls in which a shelf style layout can be built. Baseboards which fold up against the wall are another solution if your garage must also house the family car. Being long and thin means that an end-to-end configuration is the only real choice, unless working in N gauge or OO9 narrow gauge where tighter radius curves may not be a problem. This pair of plans offers a couple of starter ideas for layouts along one wall of the garage. The first (plan 21) is a traditional steam age branch line terminus with kick-back style goods yard requiring 13' of length; the second (plan 22) squeezes a lot into just 10' long by employing the old trick of fronting the fiddle yard area with a goods siding. This plan is principally designed for a more modern scheme in which DMUs operate passenger services and BR Railfreight era air-braked vans and wagons are used for the freight activities.

Above
Finger Post 2000 **by Trevor Bottomley was constructed in OO and situated along a wall of his garage. A Class 37 has charge of an engineers' train.**

Plan No. 21

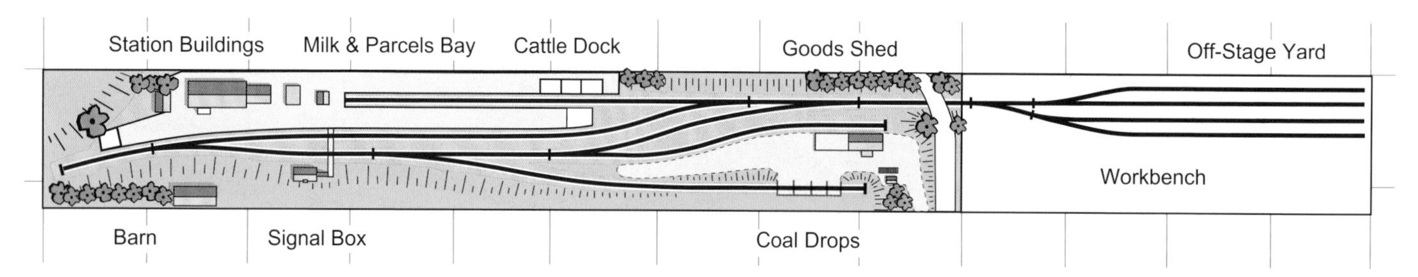

Overall size of layout in OO gauge: 13' 6" x 1' 3"

Plan No. 22

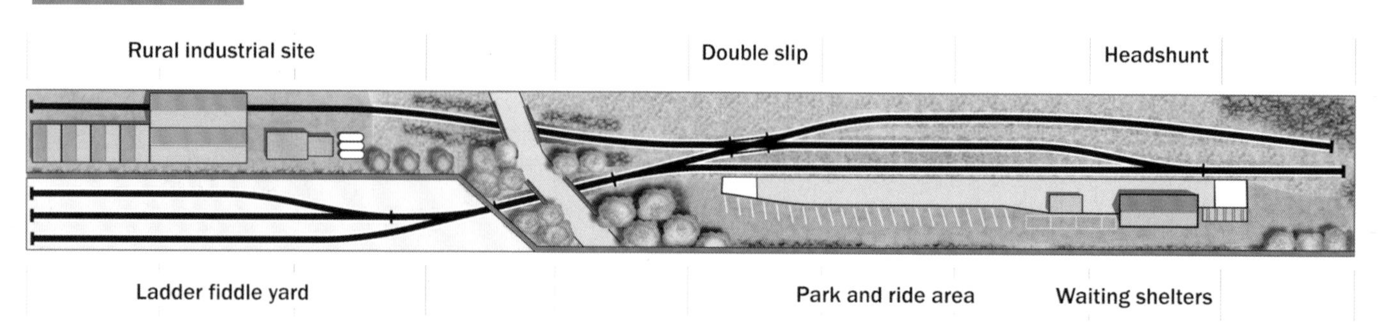

Overall size of layout in OO gauge: 10' x 1' 3"

A prototype station along the garage wall

Using the same principle, here is a plan, originally proposed by Michael Farr, which portrays the real station at Boscarne Junction as it was in the 1960s. As drawn it is slightly wider than the two schemes opposite, but there's room for a little lateral compression if need be. Although essentially a single track junction, each branch was provided with its own looped siding, hence four parallel tracks are at one's disposal; freight trains can pass passenger trains, be held in the loops, or reversed to proceed down the other branch.

The loops could also conceivably be used as exchange sidings, such that a 'through' freight on one branch could drop off wagons for a 'trip' freight on the other branch.

General goods, china clay trains and pw workings would prevail, whilst on passenger services, railbuses and perhaps an auto train or loco-hauled B set would suffice. GW panniers, small Prairies, Beattie well tanks of course, along with SR O2s and N Class Moguls, Ivatt 2-6-2Ts and perhaps a NB Class 22 diesel hydraulic (all are, or are soon to be, available R-T-R in OO) would comprise a comprehensive loco roster.

The real Boscarne Junction did not have any overbridges, just a level crossing at the west end of the site so modellers' licencing has been invoked and some overbridges to act as scenic breaks are included. A traverser fiddle yard is placed at the west end, whilst simple sector plates could be used for the east end. At 14' overall, the maximum operable train length is of two coaches plus loco, or the equivalent in goods wagons.

It's a simple rural layout with little in the way of railway structures, and thus ideal for the loco and rolling stock builder/collector. Not a plan to tax the builder's timetabling skills, but one that provides a small theatre in which to operate a collection of appropriate models.

Plan No. 23

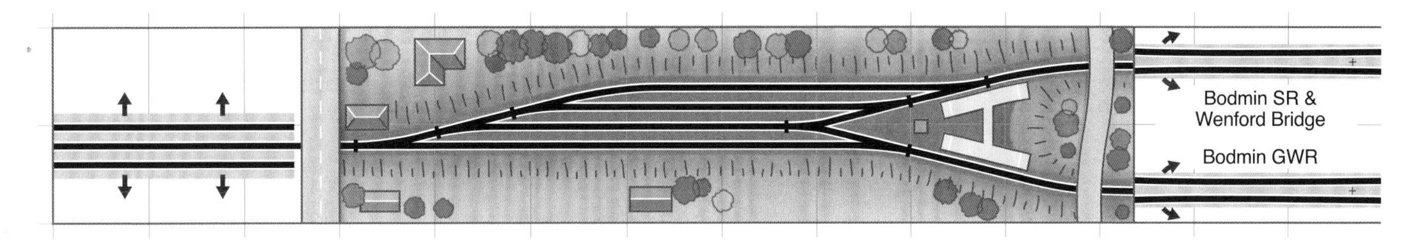

Overall size of layout in OO gauge: 14' x 2'

Below
Must-haves for any layout based on Boscarne Junction: a Beattie 2-4-0WT and china clay wagons. ***Photograph by A E Bennett/Transport Treasury***

Town sized termini

Returning to the urban theme with which this chapter began, here are two plans that are suited to suburban style services – steam age using tank engines, or modern traction in the guise of multiple unit trains. Plan 24 was initially designed with the old national network station at Bury Bolton Street in mind, in the days when Class 504 1200V dc electric multiple units provided the passenger services and the station had become the terminus of the truncated Rawtenstall route. No ready-to-run version of the 504 is available, although DC Kits offers a 4mm scale plastic kit. Naturally the plan is adaptable for any multiple unit types and includes carriage sidings for off-peak storage. One of the carriage sidings could be altered to act as a steam locomotive servicing siding if backdating the layout. An extra feature to provide an opportunity for some locomotive hauled freight traffic is the off-stage siding, which could lead to a coal depot or similar.

Plan 25 is a modern adaptation of a plan originally produced by C J Freezer. It is essentially a steam-age outer suburban station which includes some goods warehousing for perishables, parcels or other commodities that require weather protection and temporary storage. The plan is spacious and designed as a shelf-style layout around a spare room, so there is ample space for internal additions and extensions, perhaps to include a steam loco depot with turntable. Updating the plan for the present day is plausible, with the warehouse still operational for bi-modal vehicles, the coal siding is now a ballast siding, and the old mail order warehouse transformed into a Network Rail maintenance shed.

Plan No. 24

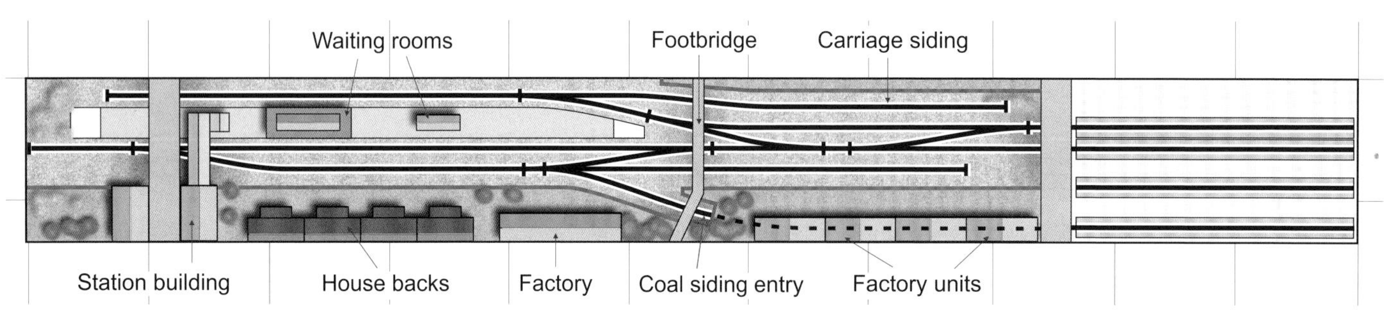

Overall size of layout in OO gauge: 11' x 1' 4"

Below
The distinctive Class 504 electric multiple units must be kitbuilt in 4mm scale, as seen here on *Holcombe Brook and Tottington*.

Above
Parcels traffic in the BR blue diesel era, exemplified by *Acacia Avenue* by Richard Slate. Below is a 'serving suggestion' of suitable OO models, available ready-to-run.

Plan No. 25

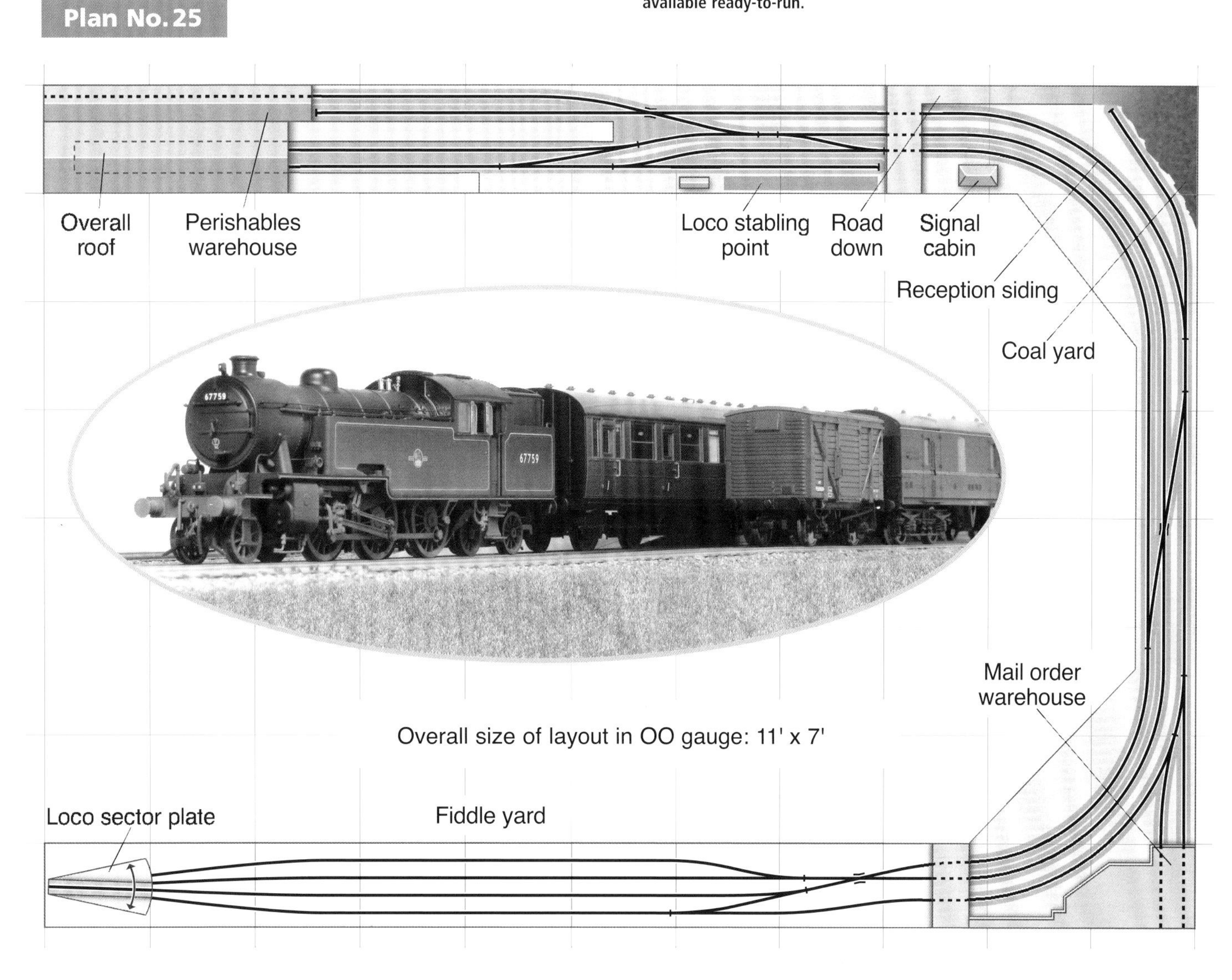

On the whisky trail

Two plans designed with the Scottish Malt Whisky industry in mind. Plan 26 depicts a through passenger station on a single track branch line somewhere in typical distillery country, such as Speyside. Only the exchange sidings for the short branch to the distillery are modelled. Traffic to and from the distillery is brought in by private shunter to be collected/delivered by the branch pick up goods, which also serves the station's public goods yard. Passenger services run back and forth as would be expected. Any period from the Edwardian era through to the transitional years prior to the Beeching closures could be portrayed convincingly.

The second scheme (plan 27) shows an actual rail-served distillery scheme which was designed and built as *Glendour Distillery* by Ian Blenkinsopp. Distilleries' traffic can include barley, coal, empty barrels and maintenance supplies inbound, with finished product, molasses and dry chaff outbound: so plenty of variety in wagon types to be modelled.

Right
Ian Blenkinsopp set his 4mm scale distillery sidings layout in the green diesel period; a Class 27 arrives with a van train. *Photograph by Phil Baggley*

Plan No. 26

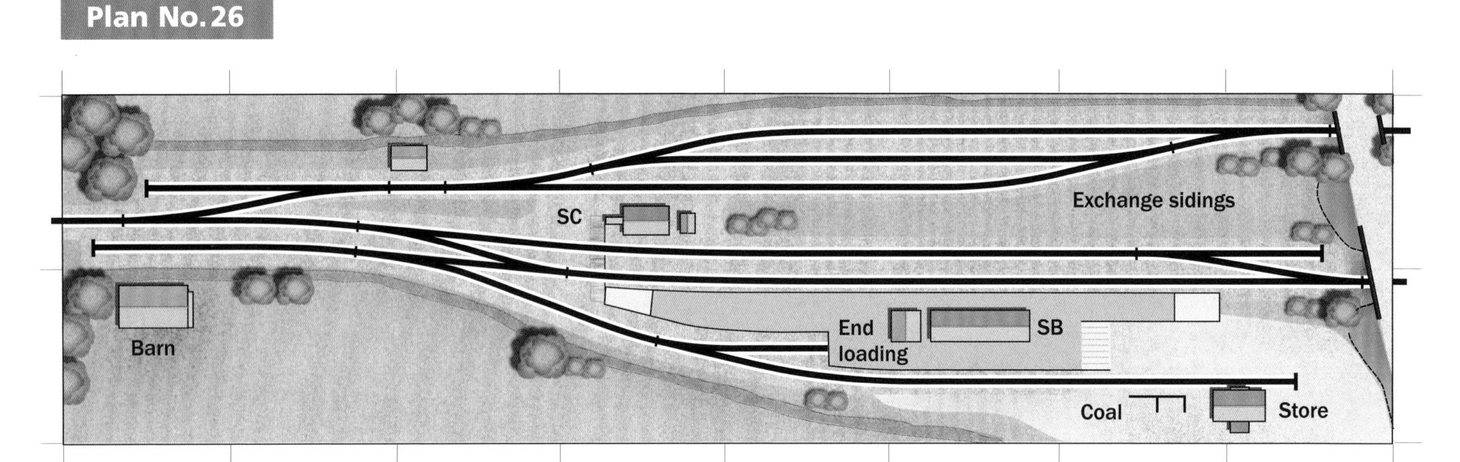

Overall size of scenic section in OO gauge: 8' x 2'

Plan No. 27

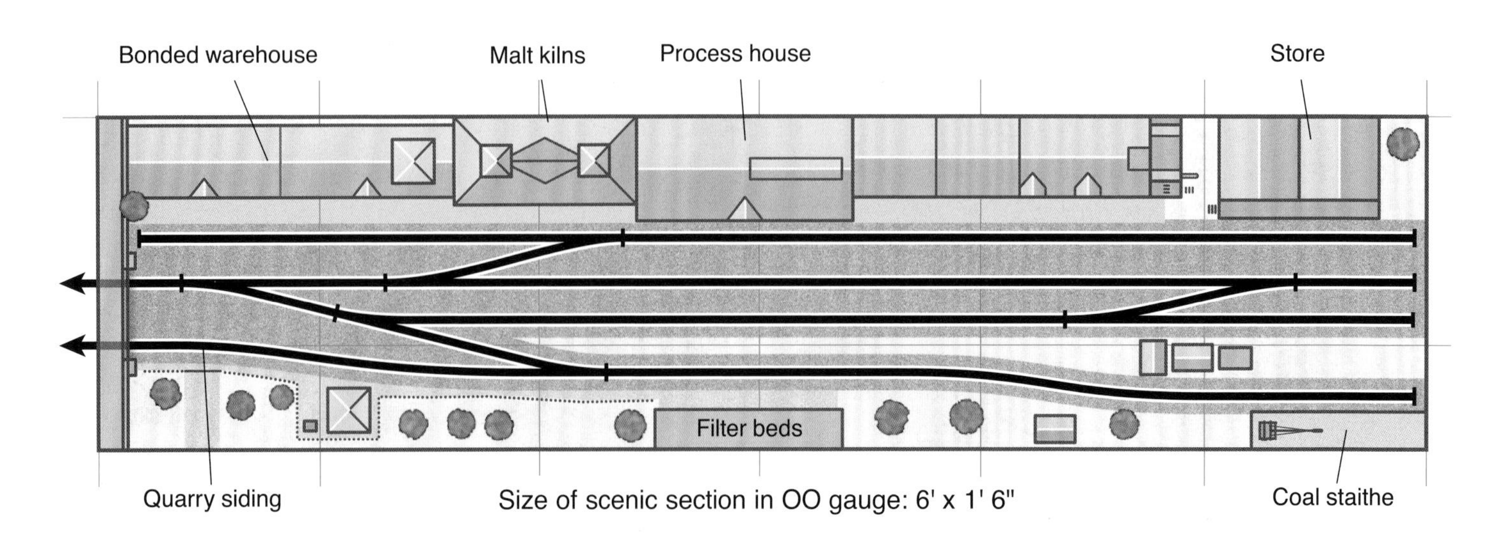

Size of scenic section in OO gauge: 6' x 1' 6"

Plan No. 28

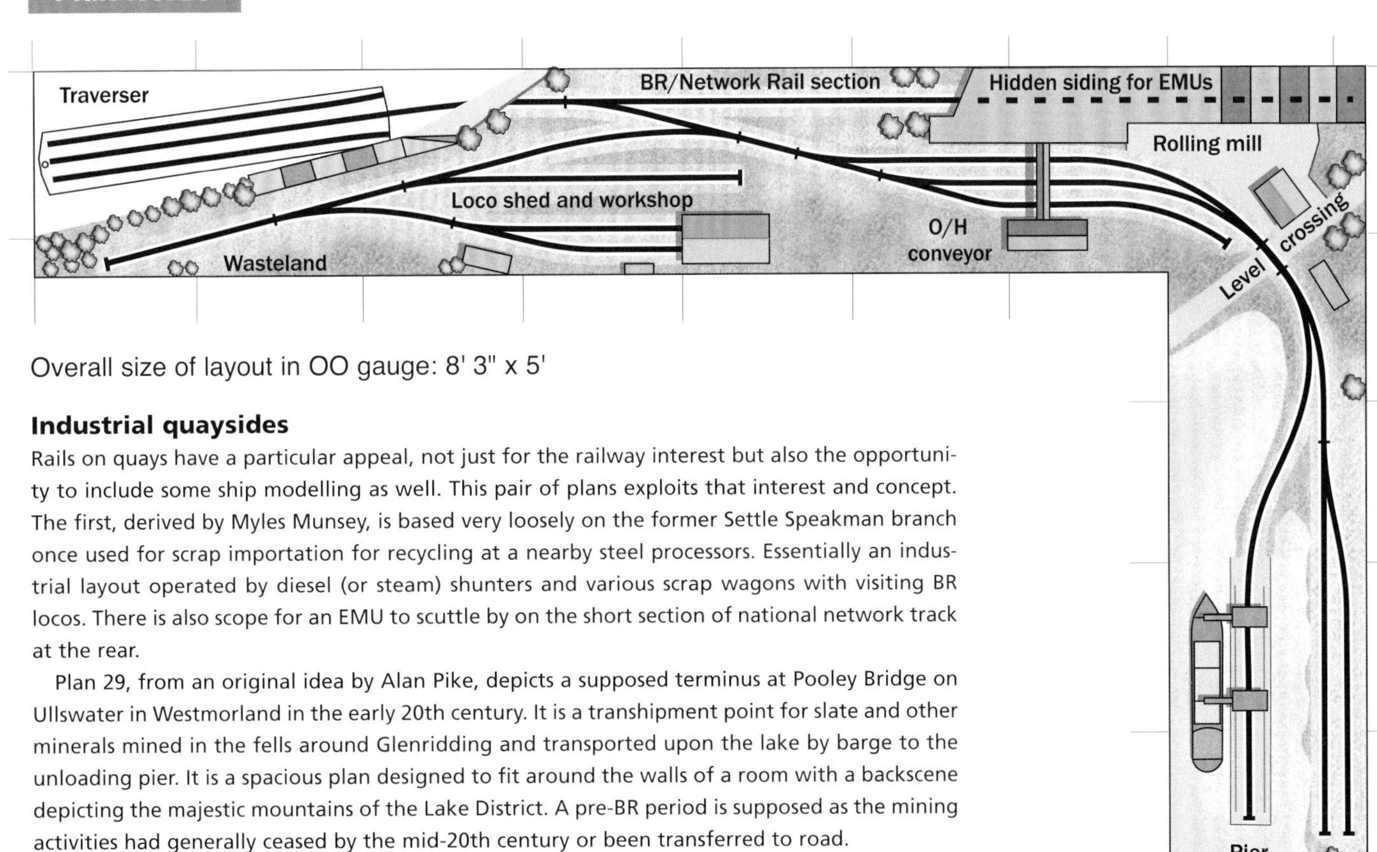

Overall size of layout in OO gauge: 8' 3" x 5'

Industrial quaysides

Rails on quays have a particular appeal, not just for the railway interest but also the opportunity to include some ship modelling as well. This pair of plans exploits that interest and concept. The first, derived by Myles Munsey, is based very loosely on the former Settle Speakman branch once used for scrap importation for recycling at a nearby steel processors. Essentially an industrial layout operated by diesel (or steam) shunters and various scrap wagons with visiting BR locos. There is also scope for an EMU to scuttle by on the short section of national network track at the rear.

Plan 29, from an original idea by Alan Pike, depicts a supposed terminus at Pooley Bridge on Ullswater in Westmorland in the early 20th century. It is a transhipment point for slate and other minerals mined in the fells around Glenridding and transported upon the lake by barge to the unloading pier. It is a spacious plan designed to fit around the walls of a room with a backscene depicting the majestic mountains of the Lake District. A pre-BR period is supposed as the mining activities had generally ceased by the mid-20th century or been transferred to road.

Plan No. 29

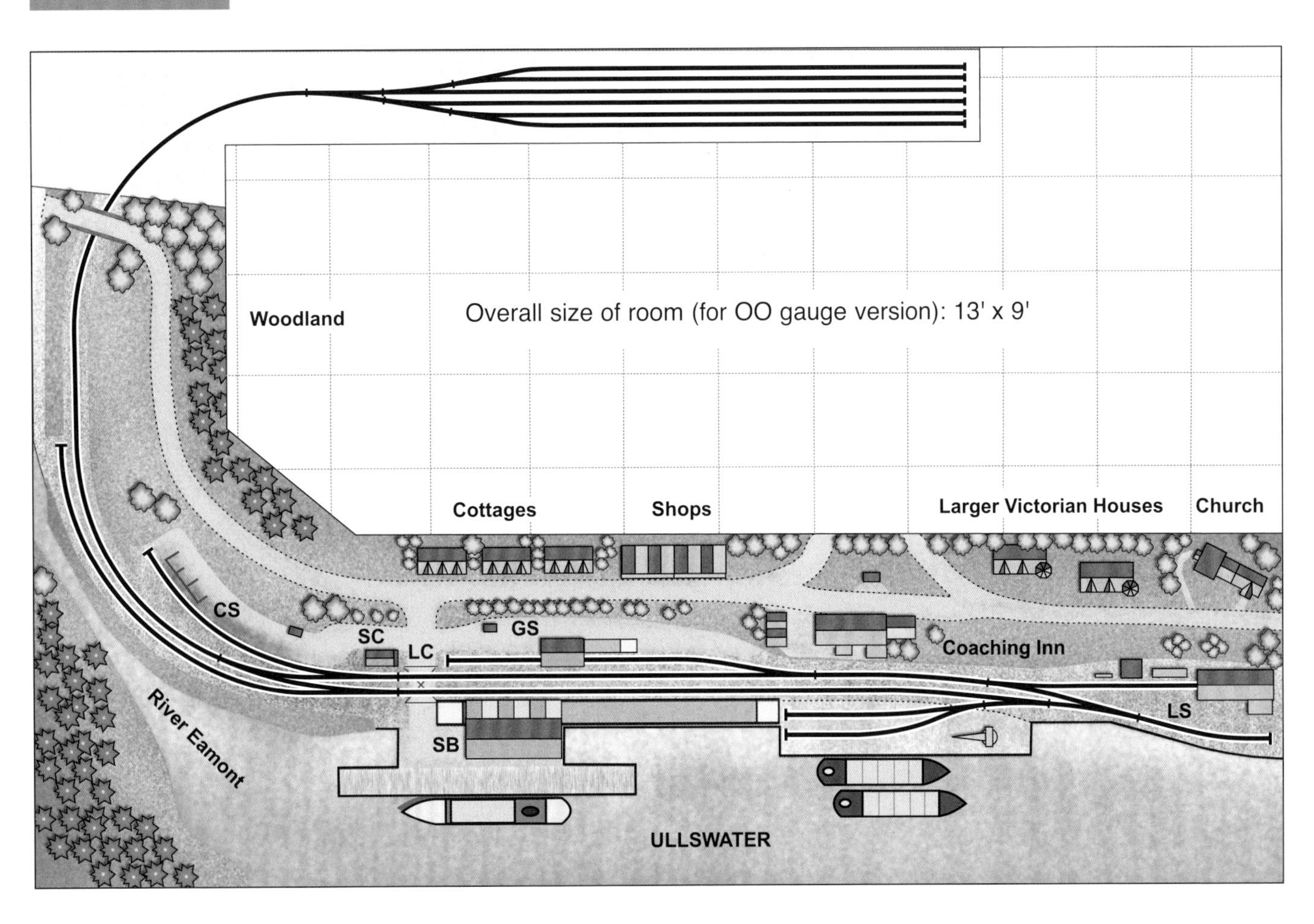

Plan No. 30

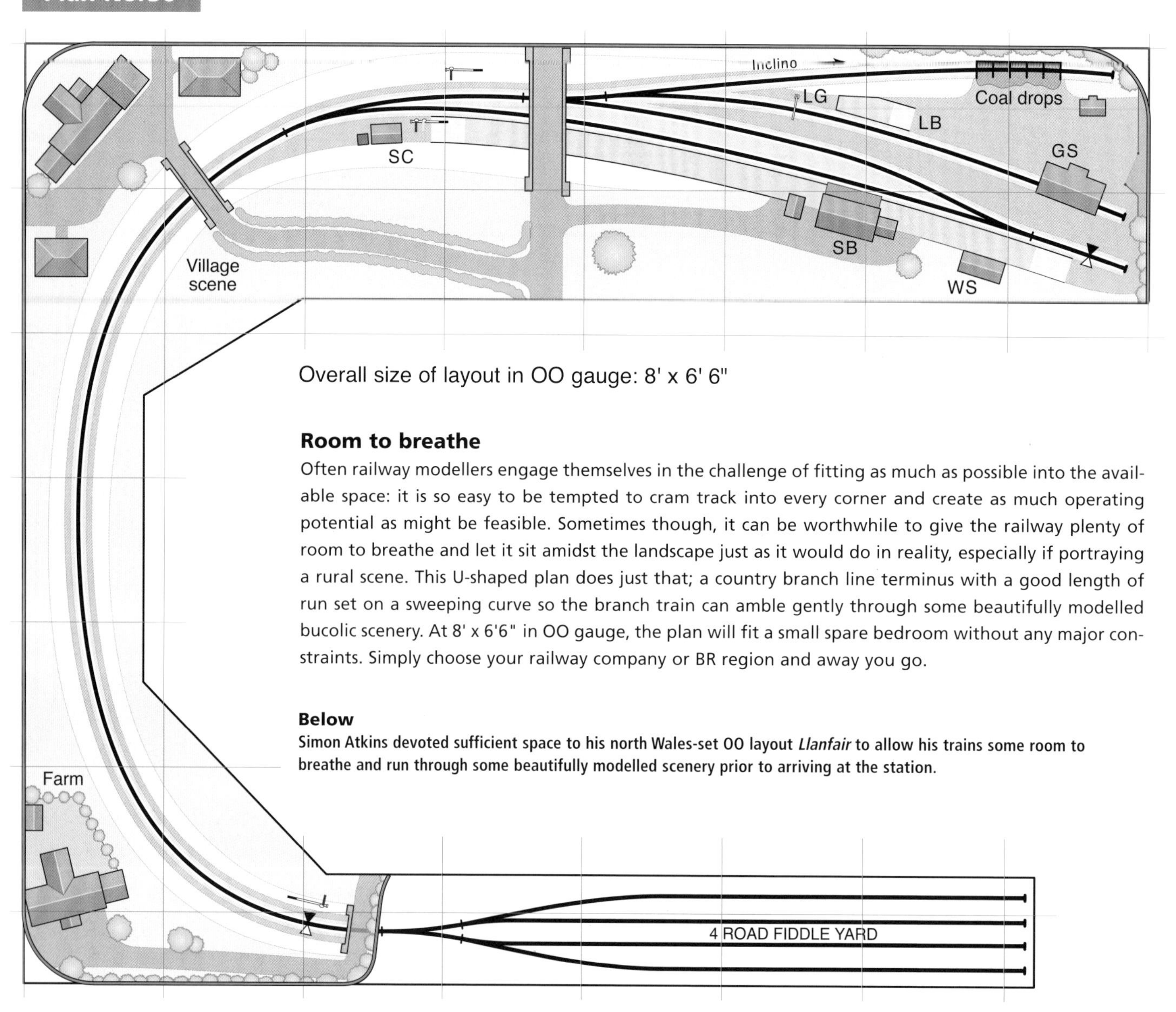

Overall size of layout in OO gauge: 8' x 6' 6"

Room to breathe

Often railway modellers engage themselves in the challenge of fitting as much as possible into the available space: it is so easy to be tempted to cram track into every corner and create as much operating potential as might be feasible. Sometimes though, it can be worthwhile to give the railway plenty of room to breathe and let it sit amidst the landscape just as it would do in reality, especially if portraying a rural scene. This U-shaped plan does just that; a country branch line terminus with a good length of run set on a sweeping curve so the branch train can amble gently through some beautifully modelled bucolic scenery. At 8' x 6'6" in OO gauge, the plan will fit a small spare bedroom without any major constraints. Simply choose your railway company or BR region and away you go.

Below

Simon Atkins devoted sufficient space to his north Wales-set OO layout *Llanfair* to allow his trains some room to breathe and run through some beautifully modelled scenery prior to arriving at the station.

Above
A two-terminus layout allows stock from different regions, periods or even – as in Anthony Bilton's railway room – countries! UK in OO on the left, Italy in HO on the right. *Photograph by Derek Shore*

Plan No. 31

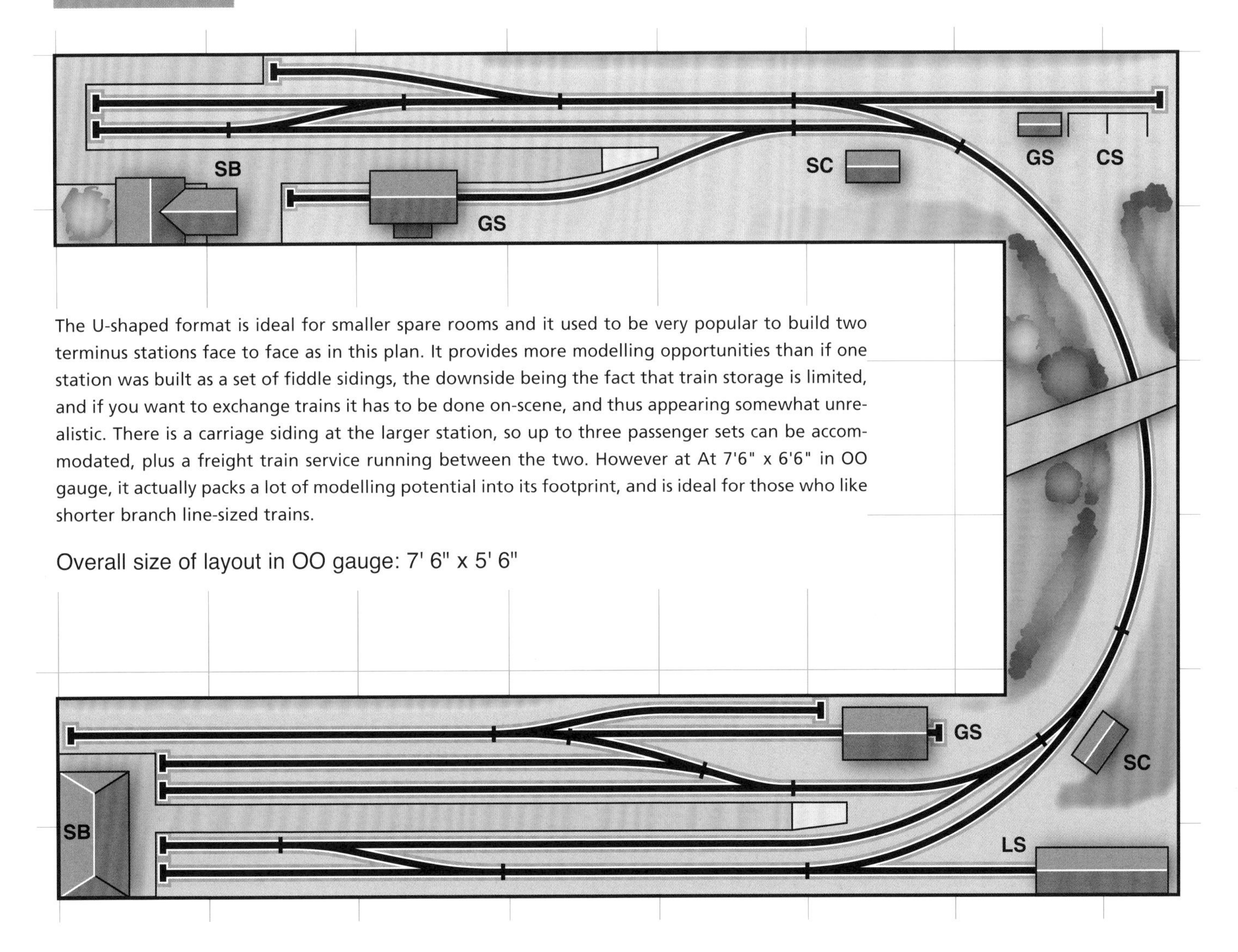

The U-shaped format is ideal for smaller spare rooms and it used to be very popular to build two terminus stations face to face as in this plan. It provides more modelling opportunities than if one station was built as a set of fiddle sidings, the downside being the fact that train storage is limited, and if you want to exchange trains it has to be done on-scene, and thus appearing somewhat unrealistic. There is a carriage siding at the larger station, so up to three passenger sets can be accommodated, plus a freight train service running between the two. However at At 7'6" x 6'6" in OO gauge, it actually packs a lot of modelling potential into its footprint, and is ideal for those who like shorter branch line-sized trains.

Overall size of layout in OO gauge: 7' 6" x 5' 6"

Homage to *Berrow*

Taking the U-shape design of the previous plan and adding a little extra width to the baseboards makes it possible to develop the idea further and increase the operating potential. Still occupying just 7'6" x 6'6" in OO gauge, we now have found some space to include some offstage sidings behind the second terminus which now becomes a small branch line to the larger branch. By sweeping the main terminus around in an arc we have introduced additional freight facilities as well. With this scheme, main train services run between the fiddle yard and the larger station whilst a smaller branch service – possibly as a mixed freight and passenger train – runs between the two stations only.

The format of Plan 32 owes its origins to a well known layout built by Mac Pyrke over 60 years ago – *The Berrow Branch* – which first appeared in Railway Modeller in September 1958. A few modifications to the 4mm/OO gauge track formation occurred over the next 10 years or so, but the characteristic single track branch atmosphere was retained. Hence Plan 33, a version of Mac Pyrke's U-shaped *Berrow*, up-scaled to get the best out of modern proprietary track geometry (Peco Streamline code 100 or code 75) and accommodate a standard 12" diameter turntable. Most of the railway facilities have been retained; bay platform, goods sidings, loco shed in corner site, and smaller terminus with mill siding.

In its day, of course, *Berrow* (plan 33) was a contemporary period layout, portraying BR steam operations in the 1950s and well before the arrival of DMUs and the dreaded Beeching closures. To replicate the original appeal and operating potential of *Berrow*, moving away from that period – certainly to a time beyond the end of steam – would not be desirable. On the other hand, changing the station names and location would not be so problematic, as any of the British Railways regions could be featured; Isle of Purbeck, Southern Region (ex-LSWR), or perhaps Lakeland, London Midland Region (ex-LNWR or FR) for example; both sufficiently pastoral to capture the spirit of the original. The builder said that he chose the former S&DJR instead of the GWR because, "one can tire of so much chocolate and cream." It seems that even then, the GWR branch line terminus was bemoaned as overdone!

Below right
A Johnson 1P 0-4-4T sets out from Berrow station as a 2P reverses off the turntable at the terminus's compact MPD. Mac Pyrke's classic OO layout appeared many times in Railway Modeller from the late 1950s.
Photograph by Brian Monaghan

Plan No. 32

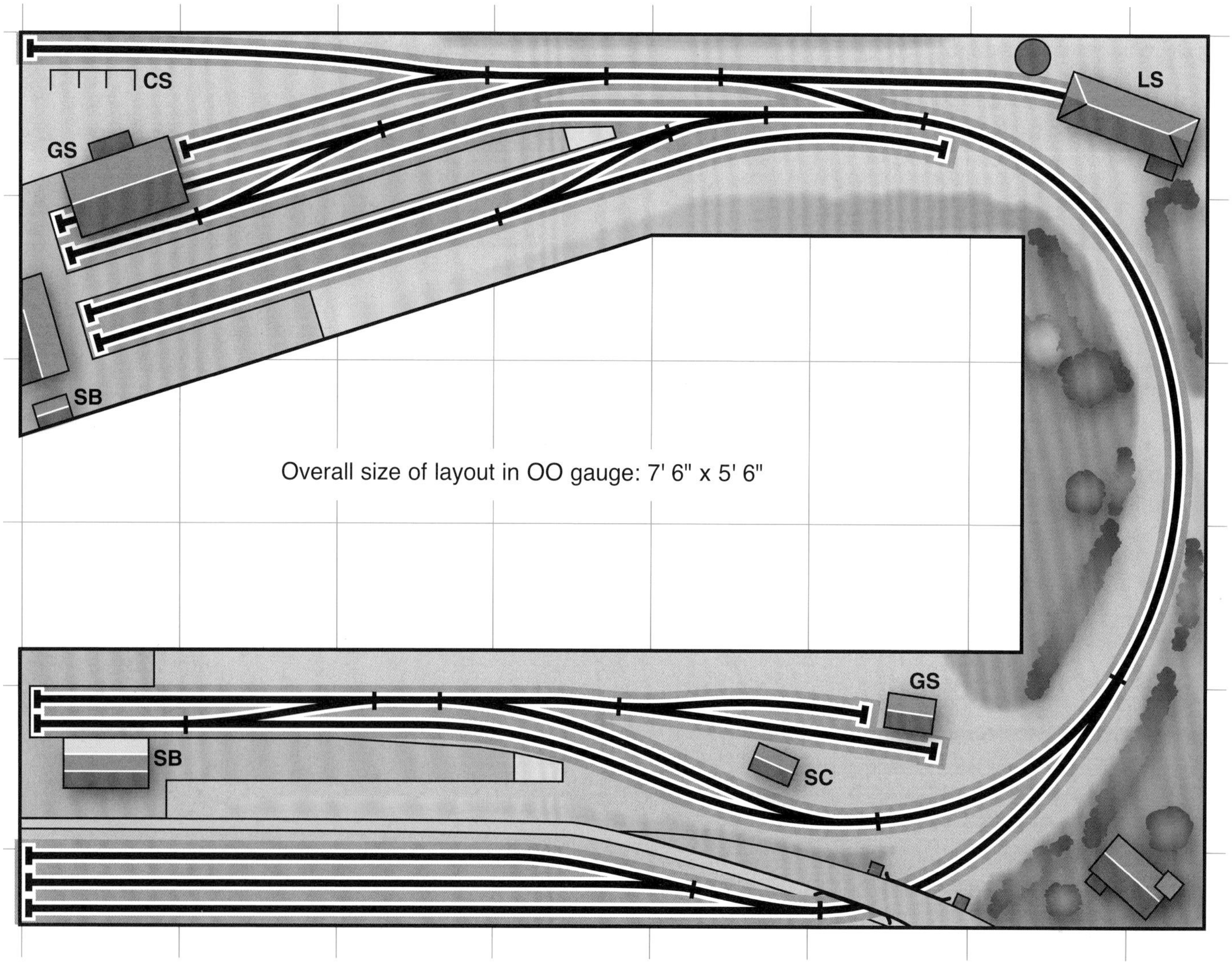

CS
GS
LS
SB
Overall size of layout in OO gauge: 7' 6" x 5' 6"
GS
SB
SC

Plan No. 33

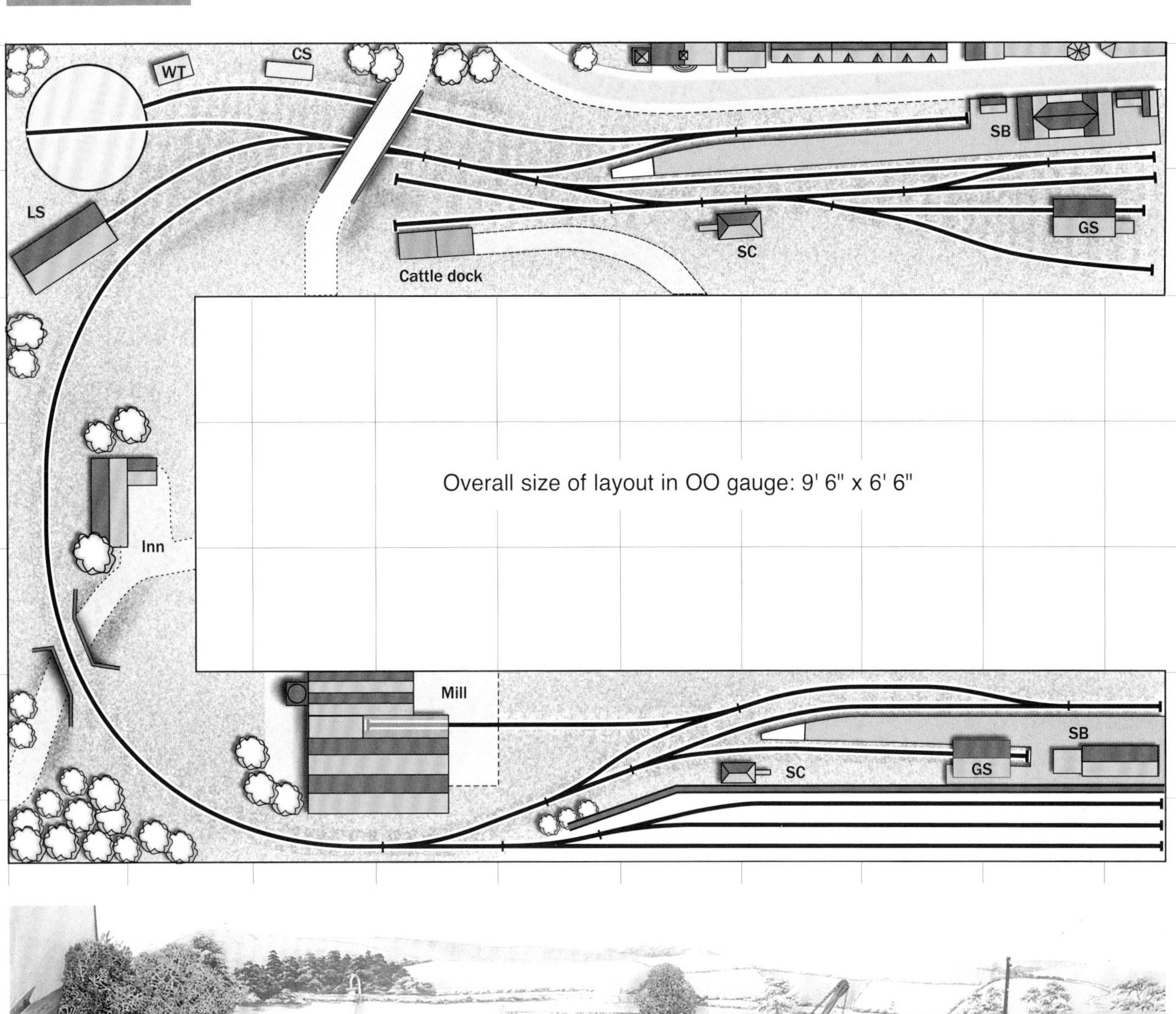

CS
WT
LS
SB
GS
SC
Cattle dock
Overall size of layout in OO gauge: 9' 6" x 6' 6"
Inn
Mill
SB
GS
SC

Traditional or modern?

To bring this chapter on end-to-end designs to a close, we take a look at two plans that clearly define their historical periods. Plan 34 is very much rooted in the steam age and depicts a typical market town terminus with all the attendant features that one might expect; twin platform faces around a centre island platform, with a small overall roof or train shed. A goods shed and loading dock for perishables, parcels, horse boxes, etc; a cattle dock and coal siding, in this case a raised set of coal drops; small loco shed with turntable and two long run-round loops incorporated in the sweeping curve. There's even room for a private siding which in its heyday may have served the town's gas works – an old favourite of those modellers old enough to remember them!

In order to fit the scheme into a spare bedroom we imagine that there is a fold-down flap to allow the room door to open or close, and that the fiddle yard is a fold-away unit which is erected along the hall or landing for operating sessions. As the plan stands, it would be suited better to shorter locos such as 4-4-0s, 2-6-0s, 0-6-0s and tank engines, though if built in a larger space, Pacific-sized engines and main line coaching stock could be accommodated if desired.

Plan No. 34

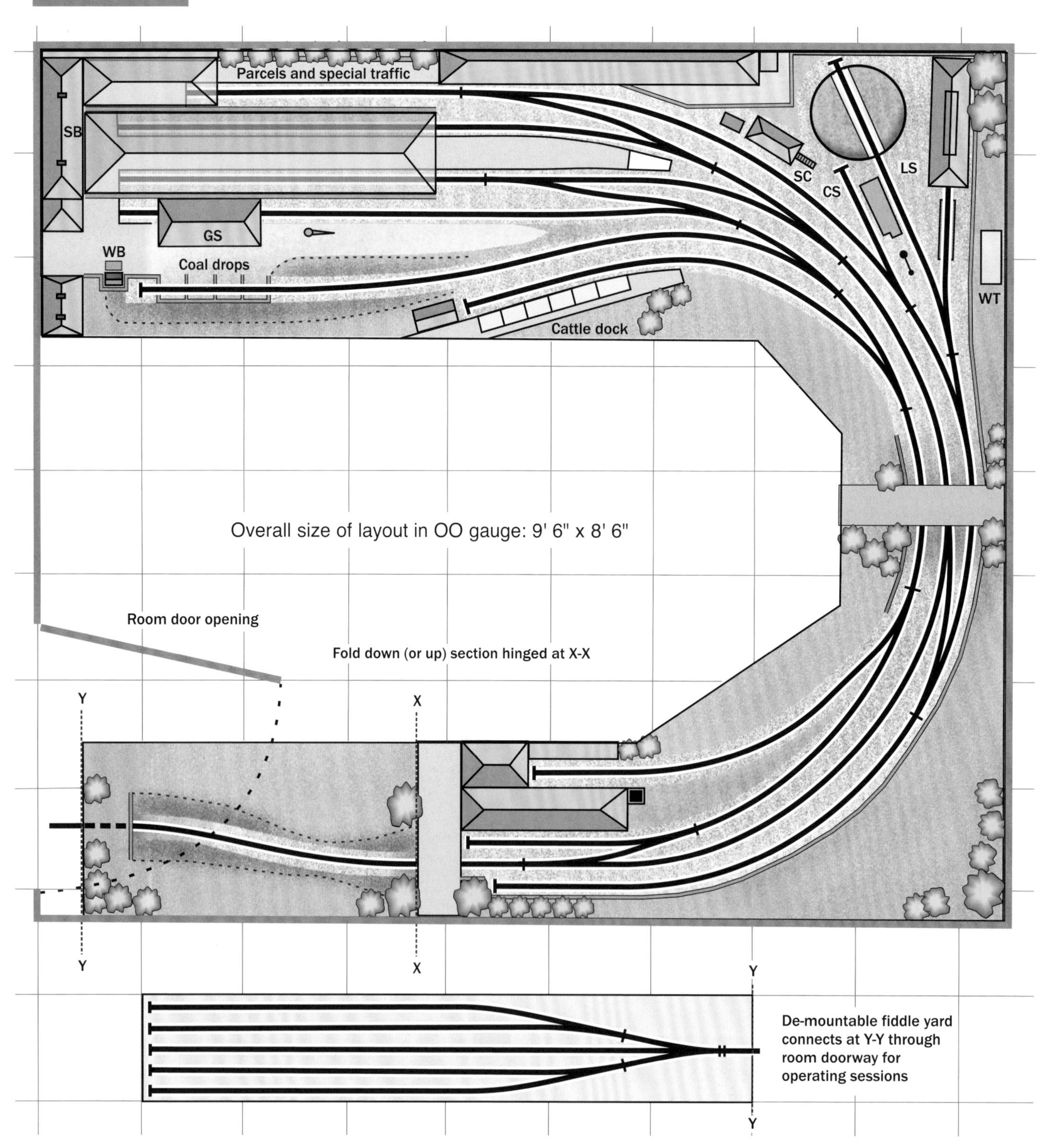

In contrast to the steam-based plan, Plan 35 – *Fambridge to Southminster* – depicts an actual prototype branch line in the modern idiom, and as can be seen the gradual demise of railway freight facilities has taken its toll. We now have just rationalised passenger facilities at both stations, and a single siding facility for the road/rail interchange of nuclear flasks in connection with the nearby Bradwell nuclear power station. Although the plant ceased generating in 2002, the facility has remained in use for the process of decommissioning over many years. The line is electrified to 25kV overhead standards and Class 307s EMUs were used initially on the branch with Class 37s diagrammed for the nuclear flask trains. No kit or ready-to-run model of the Class 307 is available at present. Today, services are provided by Class 321 four-car EMUs and models of these units are available as 4mm kits in the Bratchell Models range. Plan 35 is essentially a shelf design, and as it is presented would probably be best suited to a garage.

Foot of page
No.321 449 awaits departure time at Southminster in 2005. Few modern 25kV EMUs are available ready-to-run, but kits for the 321s are available.

Plan No. 35

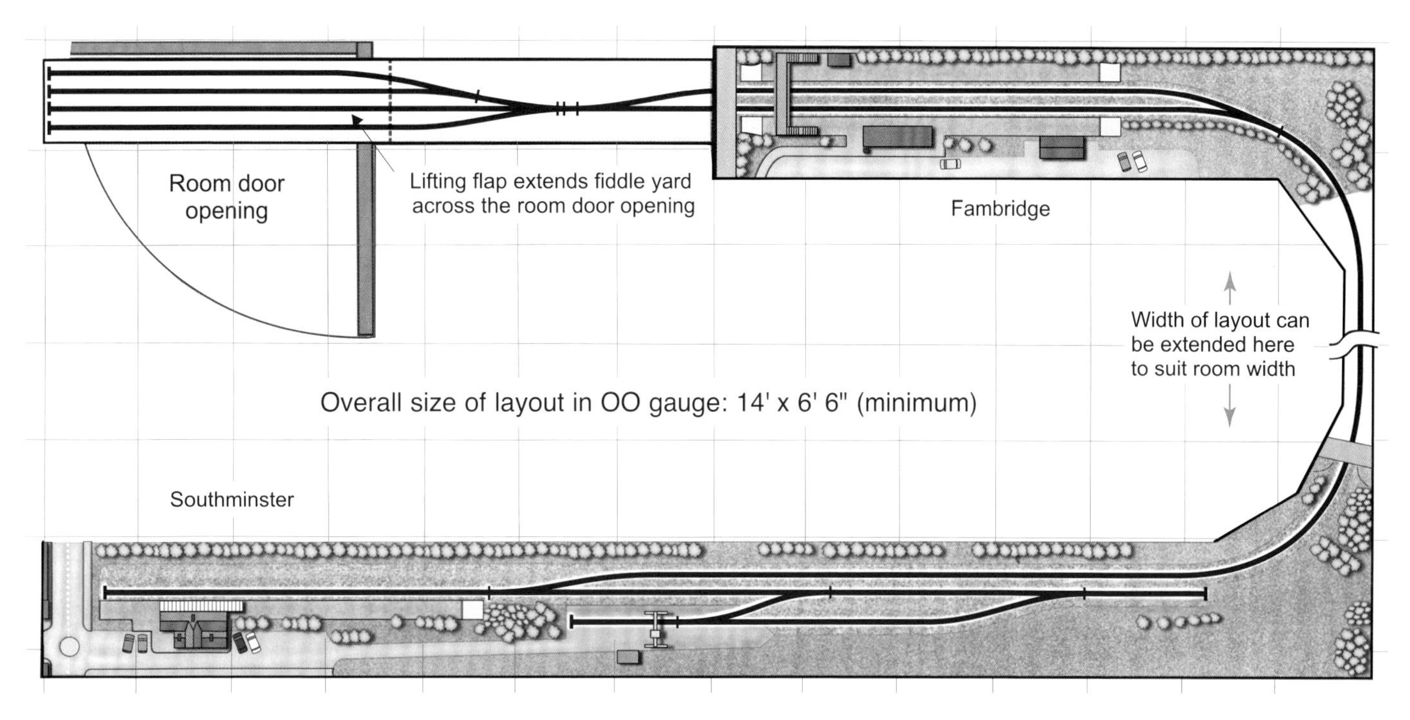

Chapter 5

Larger continuous run plans

So far in this book it has been assumed that we must consider designing layouts to fit smaller spaces found within the home. Some modellers however are luckier than others, it seems, and can devote large rooms, cellars, attics and converted loft spaces to their hobby. Typically such spaces can be around 20' x 16' or even larger, and whilst that ever present temptation exists to fill all the area with track, it is again wise to take it steady in the first instance, lest the grand project should become a millstone around one's neck!

Of course space is all relative to the scale in which you work. Look back at some of the schemes already reviewed in this book and whilst Plan 34, for example, occupies just 9'6" x 8'3" in OO gauge, in O gauge, the same layout plan would require 16'7½" x 14'5¼" – already approaching the area occupied by some of the OO schemes in this chapter. Plan 39, if built in 7mm scale, would work out at 28' x 17'6" and that's gradually becoming barn-sized! On the other hand scaling them down to N gauge would result in Plan 39 needing an area of only 8' x 5' – quite manageable in a small spare room.

In this respect 'larger continuous run layouts' means designs that are just that – larger in relative terms to the chosen scale in which you are working.

Plan No. 36

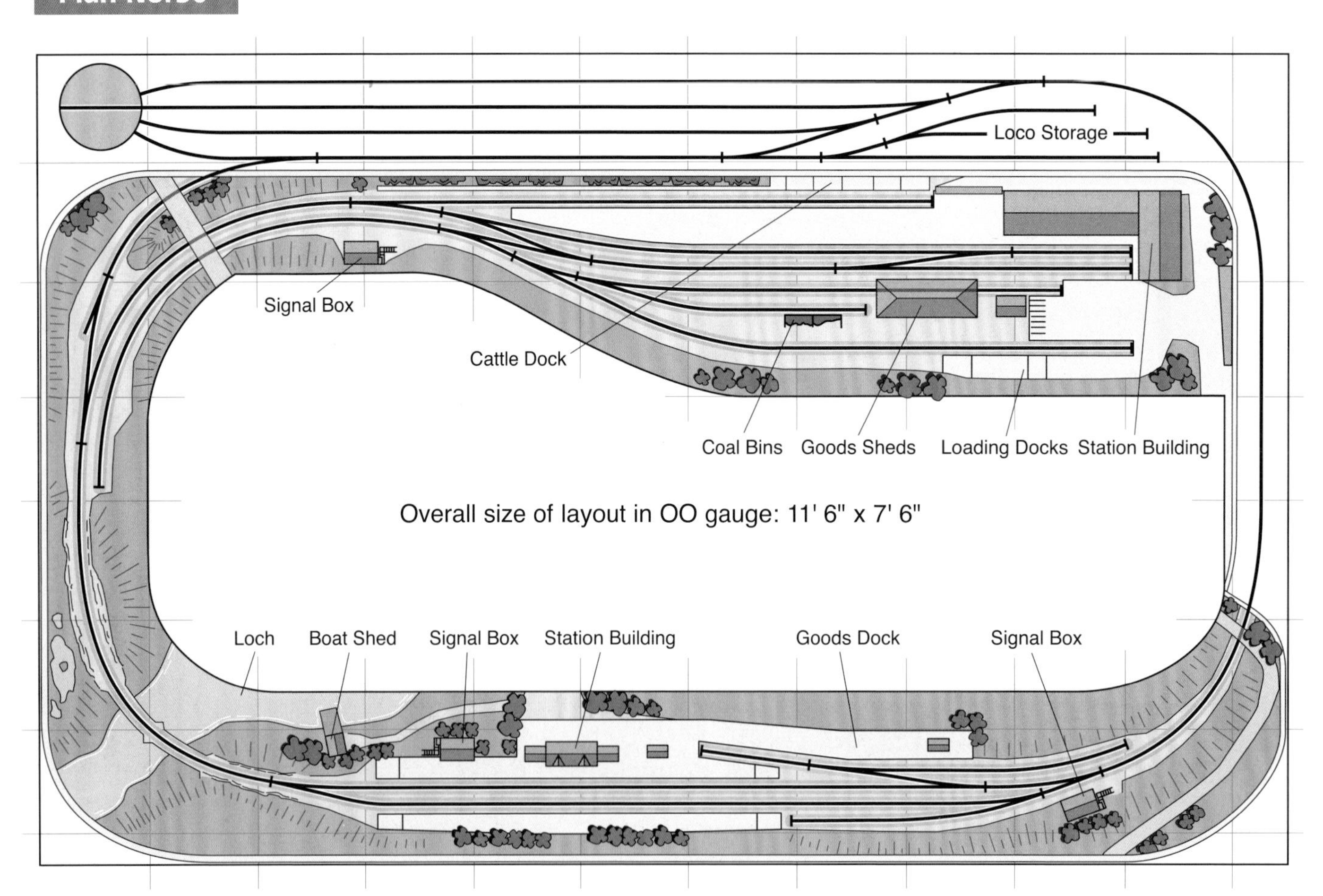

Deane Town

Quite whether this plan should appear in a chapter about continuous run layouts is a matter of conjecture, since an initial glimpse will suggest that it is an end-to-end railway. Closer inspection will reveal that there is actually a continuous run facility – one which is carefully disguised as a branch to an off-scene siding, but which in reality links into the fiddle yard, such that it is possible to run trains continually if desired. The origins of this arrangement are attributed to Maurice Deane, a modeller hailing from the 1940s, who used it in his designs. It's a useful 'trick', and hiding the fiddle yard behind the main station in this way helps save space – the only issue is access to the hidden sidings if the scenic baseboard section is wide; so bear this in mind when adapting this arrangement.

From an authenticity viewpoint, we may suppose the track running offstage could lead to the loco depot (ie those storage sidings marked 'loco storage') or a quayside, or other freight only branch. The actual track plan will be redolent of a town terminus; in this case it was originally supposed as a Highland Railway terminus, though any railway company or pre-Beeching BR region could be depicted, and the track configuration adjusted in accordance with the usual practice of the chosen company or region.

The scheme as drawn for OO gauge is quite compact, with minimum curves at 18" radius for the off-stage sections, with 2'6" radius used in the scenic sections. Although it would fit around the walls of a room or shed, remember that access to the hidden sidings needs to be considered when deciding where to house the layout.

Plan No. 37

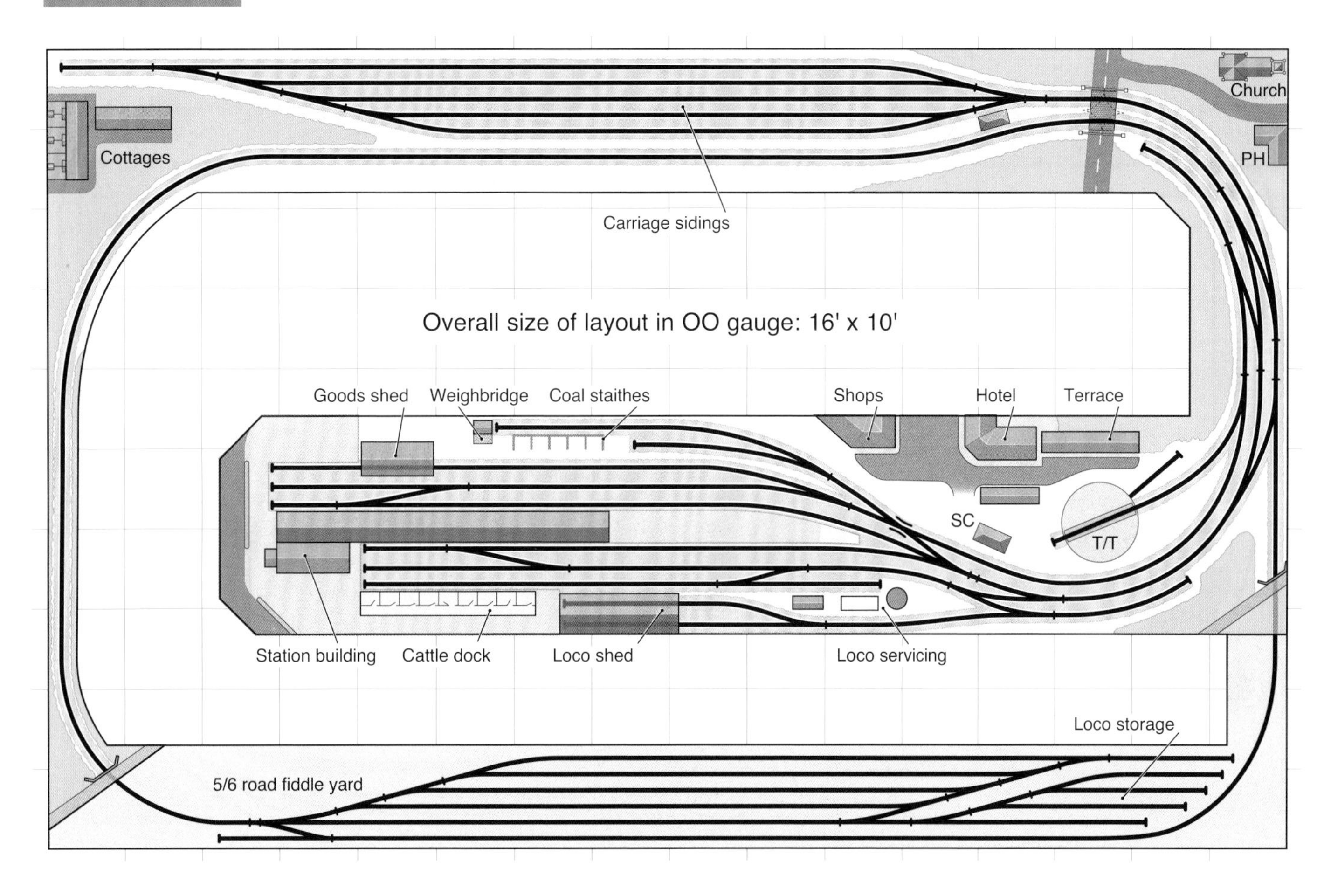

Summer Saturdays

This scheme further utilises the Deane arrangement, which is used in this larger plan which represents a seaside town in the 1950s. Inspired by Minehead in Somerset we have a single track branch leading to a substantial passenger terminus with carriage sidings, loco facilities and a goods yard commensurate with a small seaside town. A connection off the station throat leads through to the fiddle yard to provide the supplementary continuous run for periods when you simply want to watch the trains run by, or as with the previous plan, act as a connection to a freight only branch of your choice. Running a service that would depict passenger train activity on a summer Saturday in the days when everyone went to the seaside means that visiting engines from other regions on excursions would be quite authentic: so this is a plan that permits a large range of loco types and still retains its plausibility.

Passenger train lengths will be limited to five standard BR Mk.I coaches if the length of the plan is adhered to. Longer trains would be possible with a corresponding increase in layout length.

Above
43xx 2-6-0 No.6377 at Minehead on a return excursion to London Paddington on 16 September 1956. ***Photograph by Philip J Kelley***

Reedham Junction

Another plan based on an idea by Myles Munsey. A true continuous run layout with plenty of track passing through the scenery: in this case alongside the New Cut adjacent to the River Yare in East Anglia. The unusual station plan is a representation of that at Reedham Junction on the Norwich to Lowestoft main line from which the alternative route to Great Yarmouth via Berney Arms, branches off. The main line is modelled as the continuous loop and includes an interesting scenic feature – the swing bridge over the River Yare to the south of the town which is still fully operational. The branch route to Great Yarmouth runs off behind the main layout backscene to the fiddle yard which also reconnects into the main line, again off-stage, at the left-hand end of the layout. Although running this layout to an authentic timetable is not really feasible, it does offer the chance to run both main line and branch line trains, and the challenge of building a working model of a swing bridge. The plan depicts Reedham as it was in more recent times, backdating it to the steam age and reinstating the goods facilities should make for a very interesting historical model.

Plan No. 38

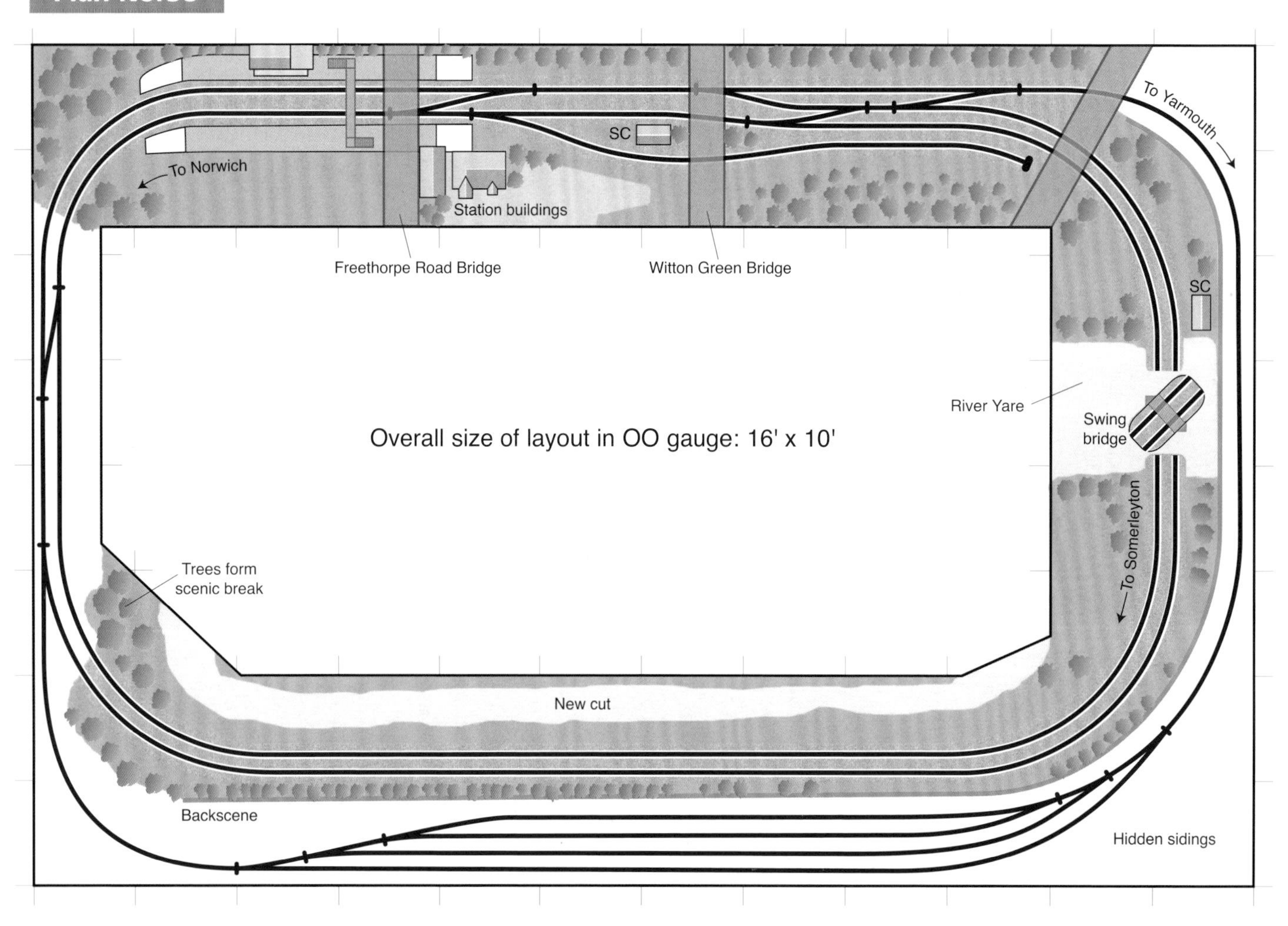

Below
The operational swing bridge at Reedham Junction, seen here open for river traffic, would make an eye-catching centrepiece of the model. *Photograph by Myles Munsey*

Dover Priory and Shakespeare Cliff

Adapting the track arrangement idea from Plan 38, *Dover Priory* is a depiction of the present station in Kent's most famous ferry port and a section of the main line to Folkestone which runs along the coast beneath the cliffs. The beauty of the station is that it has the tracks which disappear into tunnels at both ends, providing ready-made scenic breaks, and enabling the non scenic curves to be laid to the tightest practical radius. The section portraying the line under Shakespeare Cliff acts as a foil for the fiddle yard, and also provides the continuous run facility for letting the trains run through their paces. As drawn, the period is present day and would see Hitachi Class 395 Javelin high speed trains and various third rail electric EMUs. It also provides some scope for through freight workings to and from the Channel Tunnel and the addition of another set of hidden tracks behind the station backscene provides a complete continuous circuit that avoids both the station and the fiddle yard. Furthermore this enables authentic timetable running from the station, along the Shakespeare scenic section, and round into the fiddle yard without having to pass through the station again. An arrangement that would work very well under DCC computer control, where the trains and points could be programmed to run the services automatically – all without human interaction, a true 'just watching the trains go by' layout.

Right

Class 395s are dual voltage EMUs – 750V dc via the third rail, and 25kV from the overhead on HS1 – which run high-speed domestic services to the International station at St Pancras. A set is pictured at Dover in June 2010; OO gauge models were released by Hornby the same year.

Plan No. 39

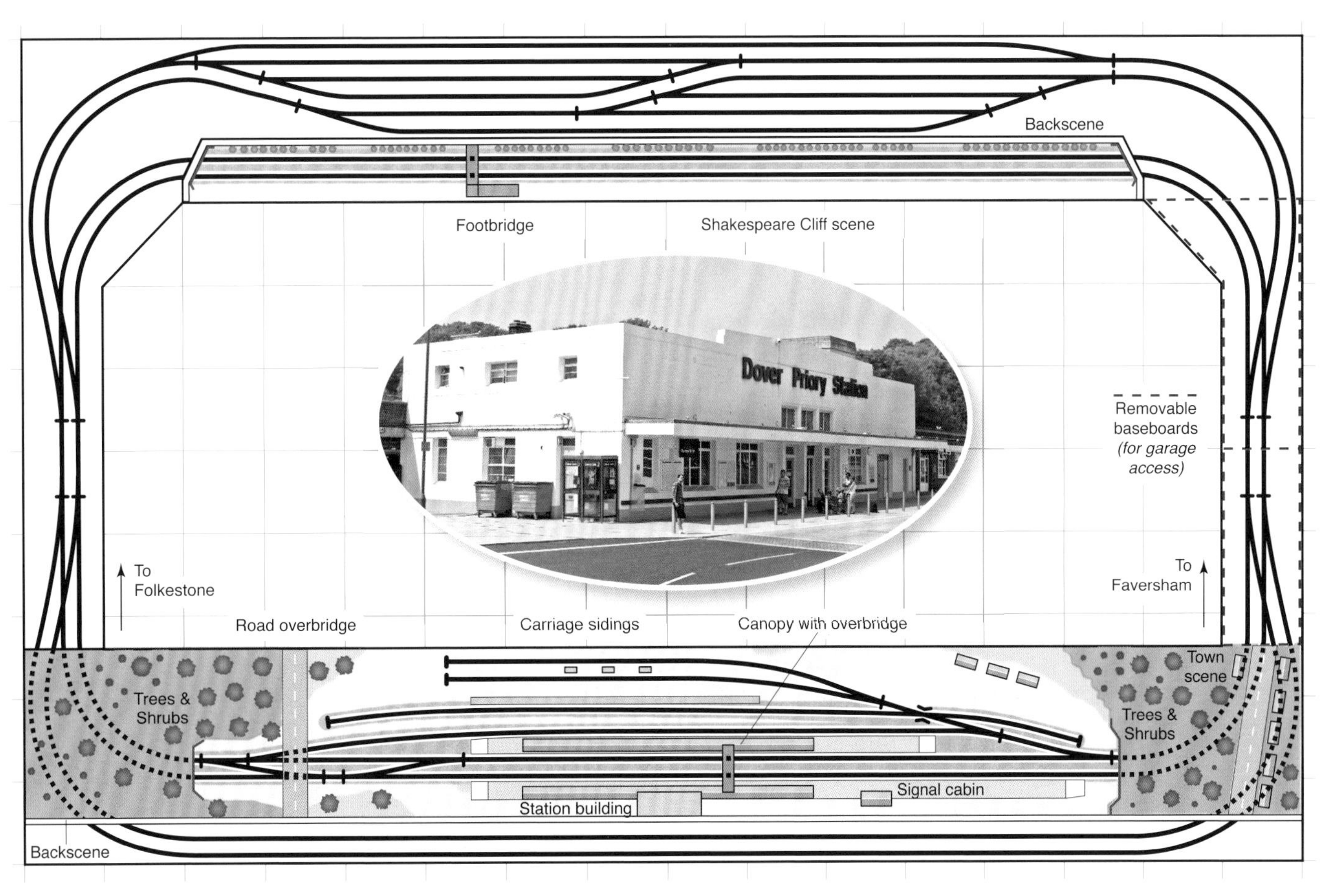

Overall size of layout in OO gauge: 16' x 10'

Chapter 6

Multi-level plans

A well-designed multi-level scheme can provide railway modellers with the best of all worlds; end-to-end operation for authentic timetable running, continuous running when you want to watch trains go by, and areas on the layout such as goods yards set aside for shunting activities. However, multi-level layouts mean gradients have to be installed to link the tracks at different heights, and this has to be taken into account at the design stage to ensure that gradients are not too steep, and sufficient clearance exists between the tracks which cross over or under each other.

The maximum or steepest gradient will be dictated by that which a model locomotive complete with its train is able to climb without slipping. There are many factors affecting locomotive performance in this respect, too numerous to discuss here, but as a general rule a maximum gradient on a layout will be in the order of 1 in 36, which equates to a 1" (25mm) rise every 36" (900mm) in horizontal distance. Obviously if you aim to run longer, heavier trains, your maximum gradient will have to be less steep, and also if the gradients are built on a curve, there will be additional friction to contend with. The other issue is clearance between levels. In OO gauge the generally accepted minimum clearance is 2½" (63mm) between rail height on the low level baseboard and underside of the higher level. This is the absolute minimum and leaves no room for overhead wires and pantographs, and certainly no room in which to allow human fingers to reach when needed. A good clearance height to adopt is 4" (102mm) – if only finger reach across a short distance is likely to be necessary – but if you want to include a set of parallel tracks in a fiddle yard underneath the main scenic boards, then a minimum clearance of 8" (203mm) is sensible in order to allow an arm to penetrate to the furthest siding when required. One should also consider a fold-down board for sections of lower level trackwork to allow for any maintenance or repair to tracks, point motors, etc, at a future date.

Incline lengths

Having established the criteria for ideal clearances between levels for OO gauge, the length or span of the required inclines between the levels can be determined. If we adopt 1:36 as being our steepest acceptable gradient, then for a 2½" (63mm) clearance, the incline will need to rise (or fall) over a horizontal distance of 36 x 2½" (63mm) = 90" (2286mm); likewise for our practical clearance of 4" the horizontal distance will be 36 x 4" (102mm) = 144" (3678mm); and our ideal clearance of 8" (200mm), the horizontal distance will be a lengthy 36 x 8" (200mm) = 288" or 24' (7315mm).

From these simple calculations we can see that the inclines have to span considerable distances so as not to exceed our target steepest practical gradient. What does this mean in reality? For hidden sidings to which access is required and which are located beneath the scenic boards (as in Fig 1 in exaggerated perspective), an 8" (200mm) clearance between the levels is preferable, hence for a target gradient of 1 in 36, the incline length from start to finish will have to be 24' or 7.315m. How this incline length is achieved will

Fig. 1
Establishing the three different levels, to allow for 8" clearance between terminus and fiddle yard (exaggerated in this view).

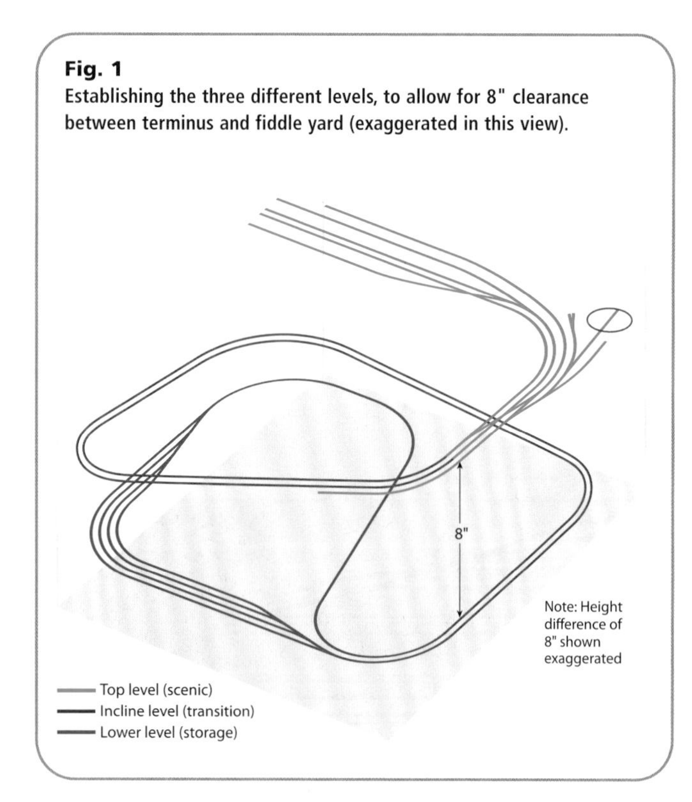

Fig. 2
Arranging the fiddle yard tracks within the footprint of the inclined track ensures easy access to the yard and any derailed stock.

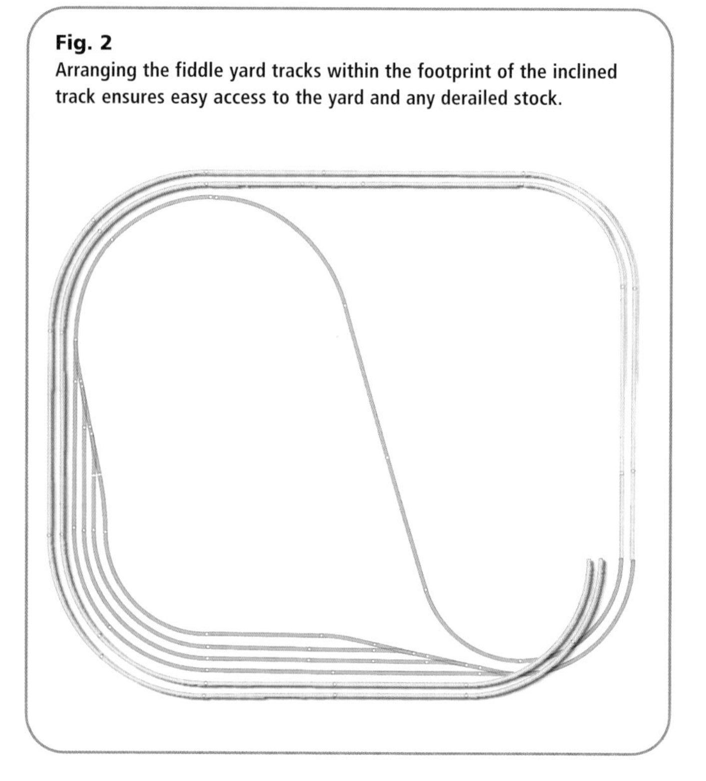

be dependent on the size of your layout room. For instance, using imperial units, a 6' x 6' room has a perimeter of 24' so one complete circuit of the room will be in the order of 24' – sufficient to give the target clearance between top and lowest levels and maintain a gradient of 1:36. as indeed illustrated in Fig 1. Of course the actual incline itself could restrict access to the lowest level return loops so these are positioned on the inside perimeter of the incline footprint – the principle is illustrated in Fig 2 and is an arrangement used for Plan 45 and similar to Plan 46 in this book.

All the plans in this chapter are designed with the aforementioned clearances in mind and gradients not any steeper than 1 in 36, and whilst some multi-level schemes can be quite complex, we begin with some plans a little simpler, and another updated version of a design from the pen of C J Freezer.

High level terminus

Plan 40 was initially drawn some 60 years ago to fit in a space of 6' x 4' using model railway equipment of the day. This modern rendering to meet our criterion of 4" (100mm) clearance between levels and to accommodate today's high quality rolling stock has been upsized to 8' x 5'. The rising incline will have to begin at point A on the plan and level off at point B, giving an average gradient of 1 in 28 – some pointwork, including that to the locoshed siding will have to be incorporated in the incline. Minimum radius on the lower level tracks will be 18".

Right
Multi-level layouts can be impressive once completed, but can be a challenge to ensure that the gradients are laid out sufficiently smoothly to ensure trains can ascend and descend with adequate performance.

Plan No. 40

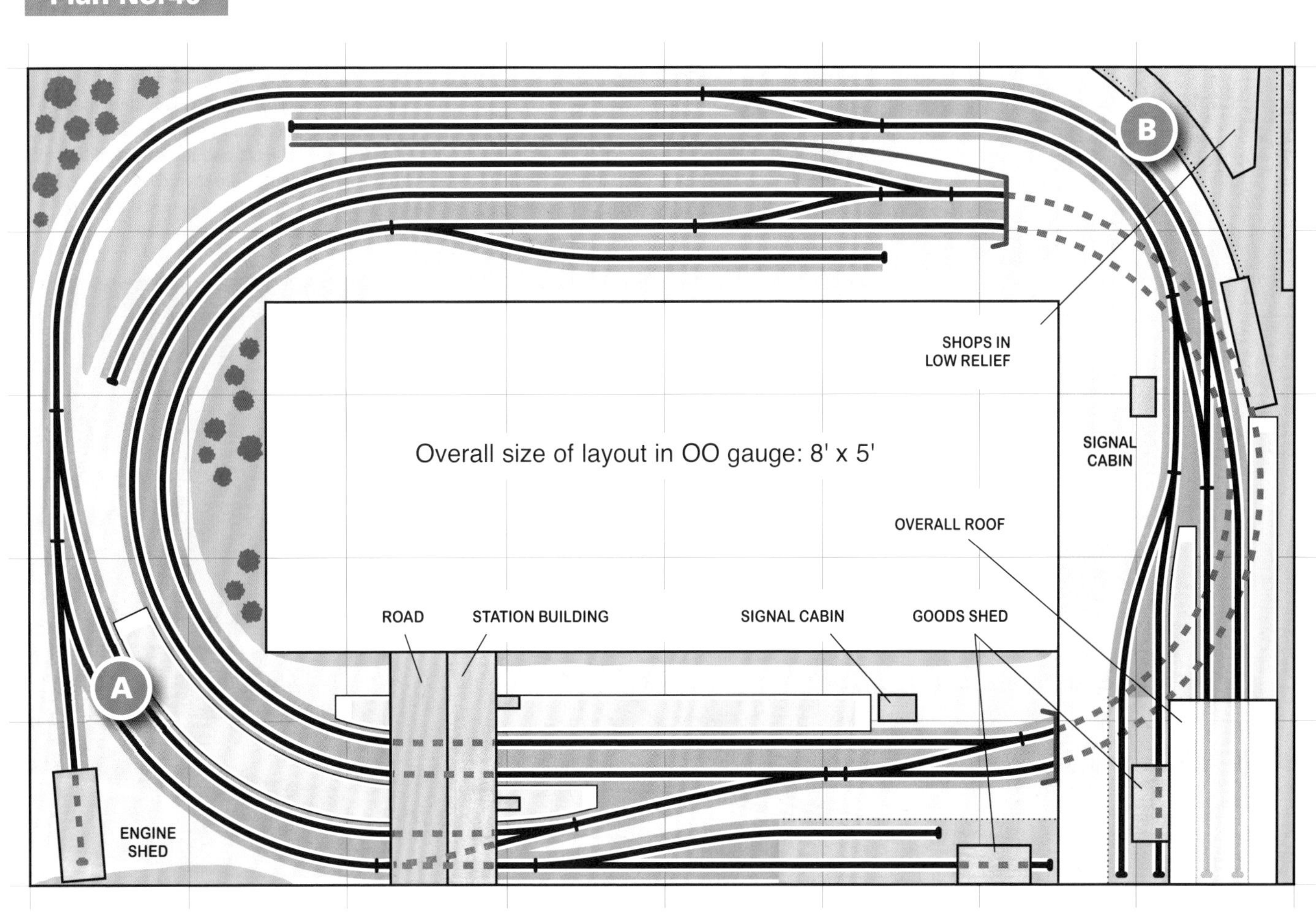

Plan No. 41

Urban Utopia

This plan develops the theme used in Plan 40. A high level terminus is linked to a low level double track continuous run via the junction station. Minimum desirable clearance of 4" and gradient of 1 in 36 are maintained. as there are no hidden loops and points – just plain track – under the high level station, a 4" clearance should be adequate when called upon to rescue any errant vehicles. In addition, an extra junction on the lower level is added to provide additional inner tracks which terminate at the junction station, providing true end-to-end running between the two termini. So lots of operating potential in a space of only 13' x 7' in OO gauge, and the inclusion of some low level goods sidings in the location suggested would add further shunting opportunities. If built to N gauge standards the central operating area would have to be dispensed with and the space filled with city scenery.

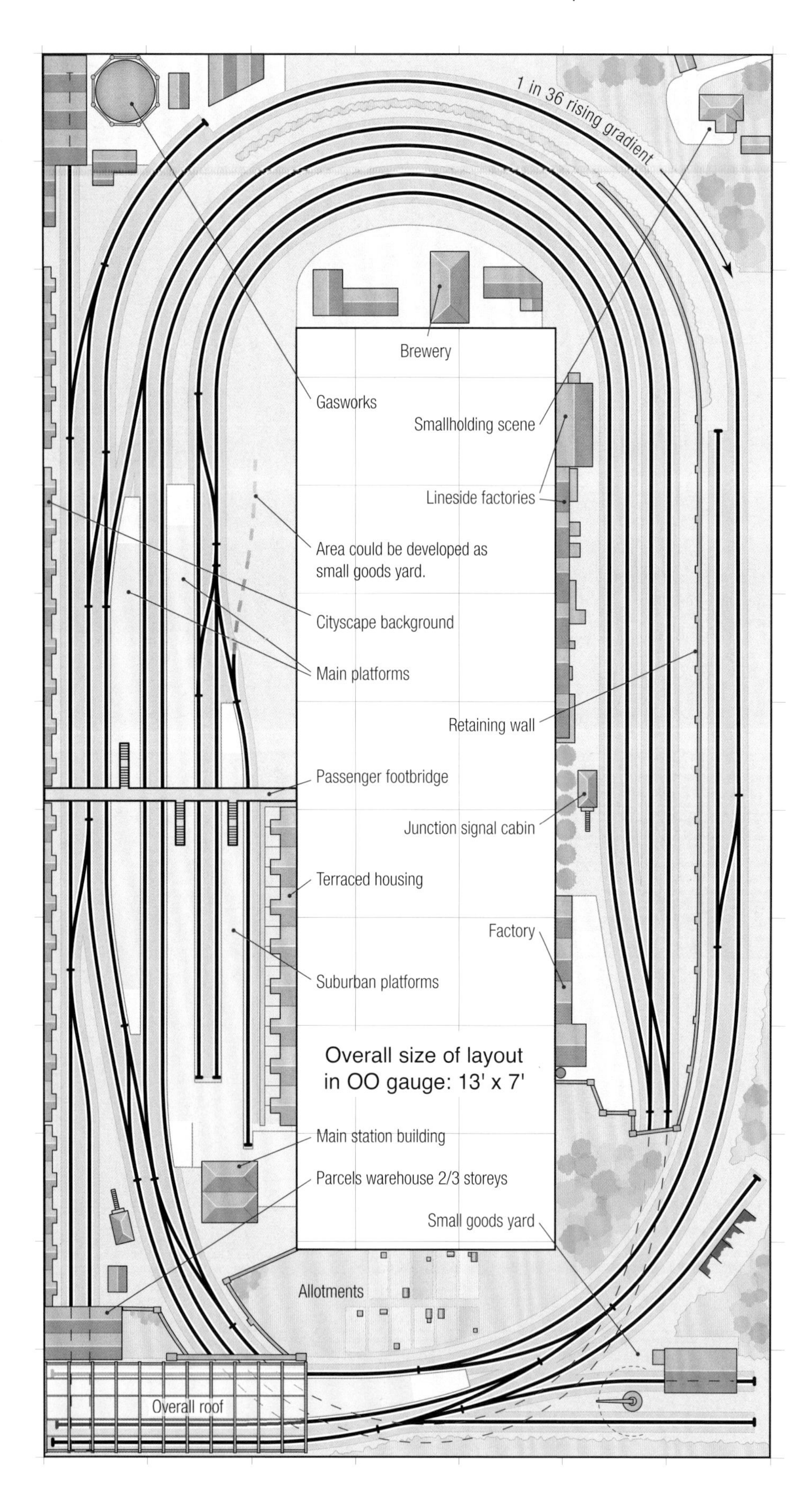

Below
Whiteacres is the extensive multi-level OO gauge layout built by members of the Stafford Railway Circle, representing modern times. Club layouts offer rich pickings for multi-level projects, and the mix of talents (design specialists, baseboard-building experts, wiring gurus etc) means that most potential pitfalls can be avoided.

Double circuit in the shed

If the construction of elaborate and complicated baseboards on multiple levels is a bit daunting, then Plan 42 may suit you better. It is in effect a looped figure of eight configuration with just a pair of tracks on a raised level overbridge. It was originally designed as an N gauge plan, and is sufficiently spacious for twelve inch to the foot operators, so upscaling for use in OO gauge or even O gauge gives plenty of scope for adjustment in relative size. There is no fiddle yard, just a fully scenic marshalling yard, used for both passenger stock and freight trains, and large locomotive depot which has independent connections to the sidings (shown in red) to minimise hold-ups on the main lines. Furthermore this is the only route by which trains can be swapped from the up main line to the down main line.

Plan No. 42

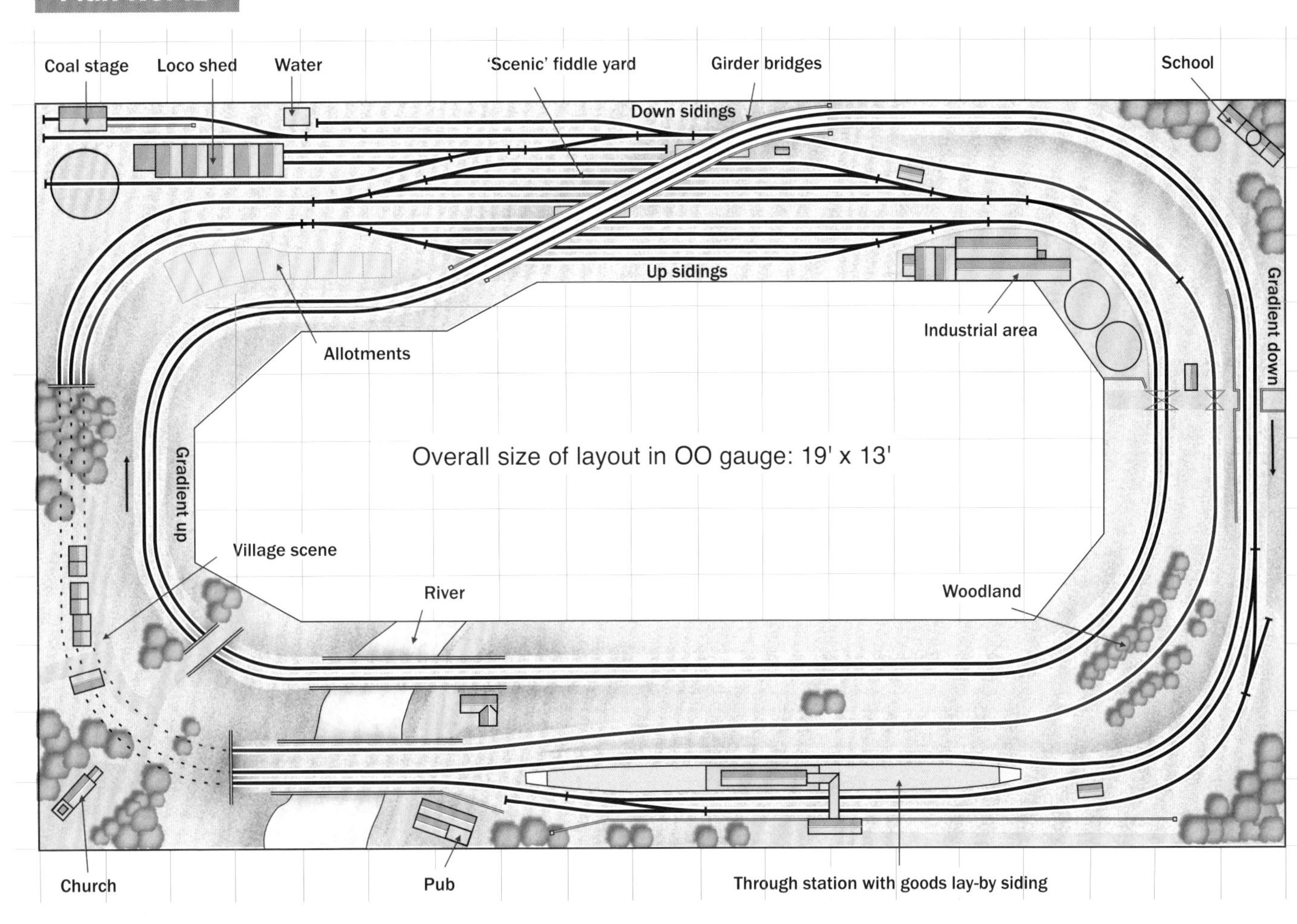

Plan No. 43

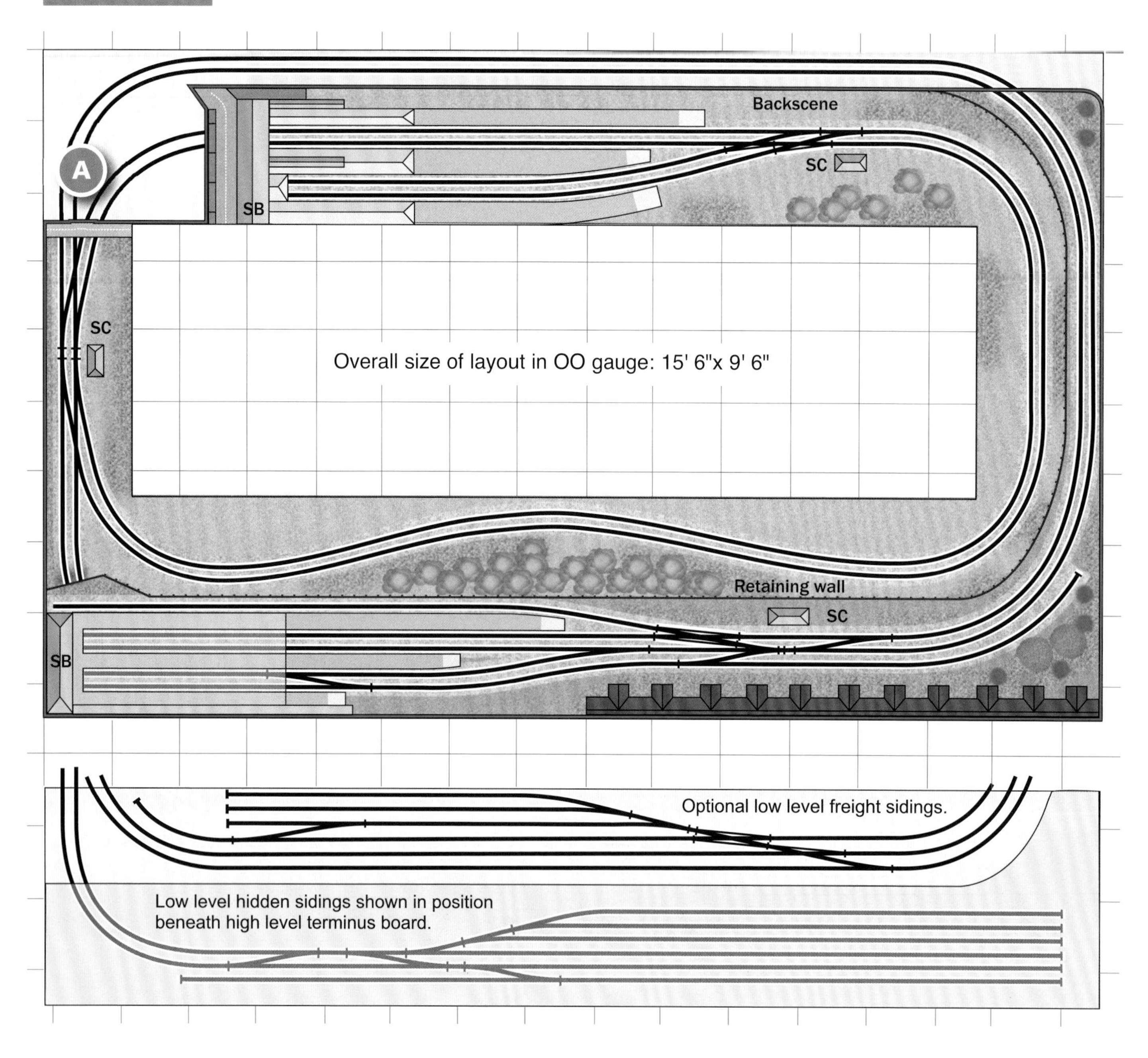

Electric Heaven

In recent times the OO gauge ready-to-run manufacturers have woken up to the Southern electric scene in a big way. Successful modelling of this genre is now within reach of many more modellers, but an important consideration has to be train length. Southern Region EMU sets can vary from two cars up to 10 cars on main line services, resulting in fairly lengthy train combinations in model form – up to 10' long in OO gauge.

This plan takes that fact into account and is thus a fairly ambitious scheme for a permanent room-size twin-level layout. There are two stations; a high level terminus and a through station with two terminus platforms, and a fairly extensive set of hidden sidings beneath the high level terminus. There is also a section of main line run with some goods sidings which gives scope for freight operations on the lower level circuit. For the gradient I have assumed a 4" clearance between the lower rail tops and the underside of the supporting cross members for the high level baseboards, which will be around 3" deep depending on the choice of top surface. Starting the incline at A on the plan gives something like 22' of steadily rising gradient at an average of 1 in 37. With slight easing of gradients on the curves, themselves to a minimum of 24" radius, today's model EMUs should cope admirably. Access to the hidden fiddle yard tracks will be quite restricted for maintenance and stock rescue in the event of a derailment, so consideration should be given to making the scenic sections of the top boards removable, or even having the whole baseboard built as hinged flap sections that can be folded upwards once the stock has been removed.

As drawn the scheme depicts a fairly rural stretch of Southern metals, allowing eight-car trains to show off their performance through the countryside. There is some scope for parcels and perishable traffic between the hidden sidings and the terminus, perhaps with the occasional van dropped off in a bay in the through station. Class 33 haulage would be typical in post-steam days, whilst Moguls and BR Standards would be seen alongside green liveried EMUs.

City Lights

Plan 44 is a 16' x 11' plan for a city themed main line to fit a room, garage or attic. There is a large passenger terminus linking into a continuous run which includes a suburban through station. A lower level incorporates a single track reversing loop to enable loco hauled trains to return to the terminus after having circulated a few times. Also on the low level section is a train maintenance depot which can accommodate full length multiple unit trains and several locos. To disguise the oval nature of the layout it is divided into separate scenes by the use of curved backscenes and various overbridges which act as view blockers.

As well as the main maintenance train shed, there is an external raised walkway for carriage servicing, a small refuelling point for diesel units and a carriage washing plant. There is no pretence that the depot feature represents an accurately researched and correct-in-every-detail design, instead, it is intended as a starting point to capture the atmosphere and spirit of the prototype.

The main line loop runs on raised arches along the back of the depot, reminiscent of urban railway landscapes in many of our crowded cities. The terminus scene is quite confined with little room for non-railway scenery. I have included a canal or riverside scenic feature which by the 1990s would have been refurbished for leisure boating use. The old towpaths would have been turned into proper footpaths, seating areas and modern street lighting would have been provided and I can even imagine one of the old railway arches being turned into a café bar! There may even be room for that old bonded warehouse that has now become transformed into a luxury penthouse apartment block.

Freight potential is modest. A rail served factory is included at the terminus end of the layout, accessed from the main lines via a single slip running into its own reception loop. Once the loco has run round its train the sidings can be shunted independently of the main lines. At the suburban station the former goods yard has been redeveloped into private sidings, probably with the aid of an old Section 8 grant. A silo has been erected to deal with some sort of bulk commodity such as cement, grain, or other powder-based mineral.

The plan has been designed with proprietary track and pointwork in mind, and curves have been set at a minimum radius of 3' (0.914m). As there are no sidings on the lower level reverse loop, we can be satisfied with minimum height clearances – say 4" (100mm), giving a maximum gradient of 1 in 36 – just! Scaling down to N gauge is perfectly possible – but watch the operating spaces as they shrink to unusable proportions. As for scaling up to O gauge, that's possible too, though finding a space 28' (8534mm) x 19'3" (5867mm) in size may not be that easy!

Plan No. 44

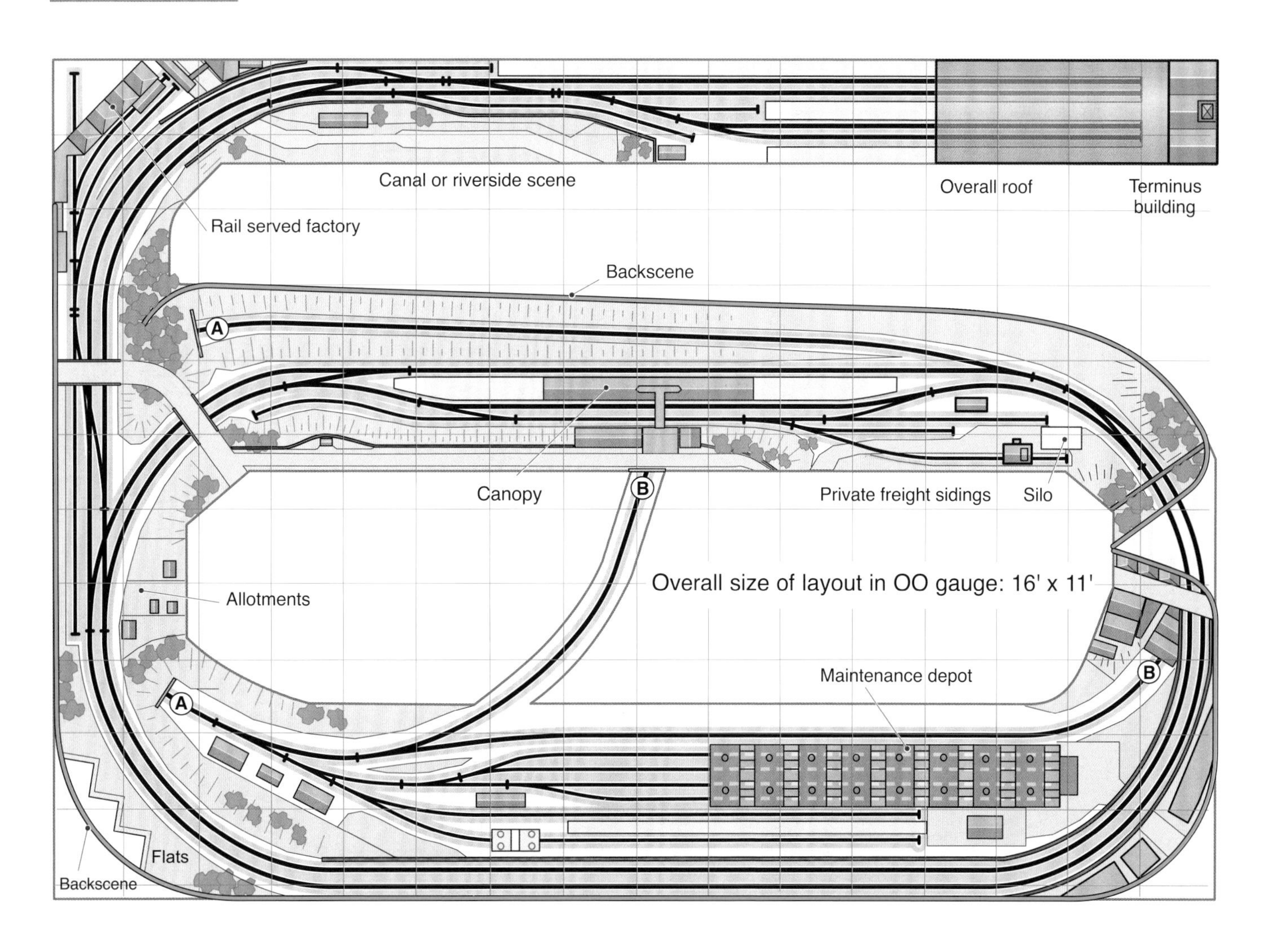

Out and back automatically

At the beginning of this chapter it was shown how an incline running around the full perimeter of a room can provide 8" clearance (for OO gauge) above a set of fiddle yard loops on the lowest level (see Fig 1 on page 38).

Plan 45 makes use of that arrangement with a country town terminus modelled on the upper level. Tracks to and from the station run around the room steadily dropping in height to reach the low level section some 8" beneath. A set of parallel storage sidings and a return loop on this lower level provide an out-and-back arrangement for all trains. The 8" of clearance also provides full access for hands and arms for retrieving errant stock or to deal with maintenance needs that crop up from time to time.

Occupying a space of only 10' x 8' means that the operating area is quite compact, especially as a length of the return loop cuts it in two as shown. This means a duck-under action, or designing a lifting section which, when raised, would have to cut power upstream of it to prevent trains coming to grief.

To make the scheme easier to follow, plan views of each of the three levels are also included opposite to help show how they all fit together, one above the other. Fig 1 shows the top level only, and includes the baseboard perimeter as seen in the main plan illustration below. The sections of track shown in green indicate the start of the falling gradient which runs around the room and is shown in full in Fig 2. Fig 3 shows the lowest level with the return loop and storage tracks. On the diagrams Peg A shows the position at which the top level tracks connect to the inclined (middle level) tracks; peg B shows the position at which the inclined tracks meet the low level storage and return loops. Note also in Fig 3 that from the position indicated by peg C, the low level tracks sit *inside* the middle level tracks, all the way to peg D; this ensures that there is always a full 8" of clearance to the low level tracks.

There is of course a slight downside to this arrangement in that a lot of running takes place out of sight, so the operator cannot fully watch trains passing through open scenery. On the other hand, trains can set out and return to the terminus station without the need to be manhandled or re-marshalled in any way. This means that some sort of automatic control of the hidden sidings could be installed, such as electronic timer circuits and infra-red train detectors, or a means of DCC computer control.

Sending trains outbound and awaiting their automatic return in this way can really reinforce the illusion that trains actually go off on a journey to be dealt with elsewhere.

Plan No. 45

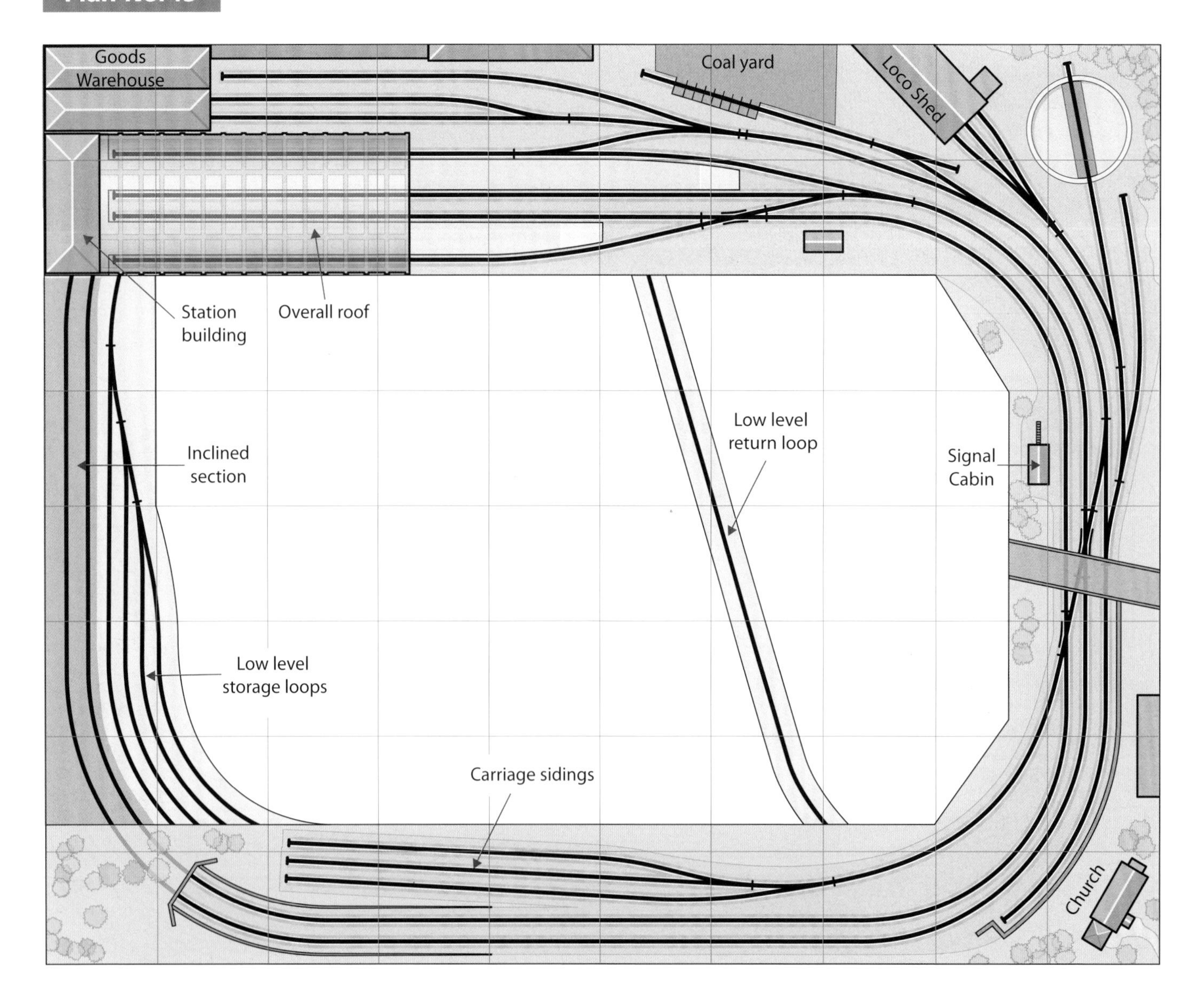

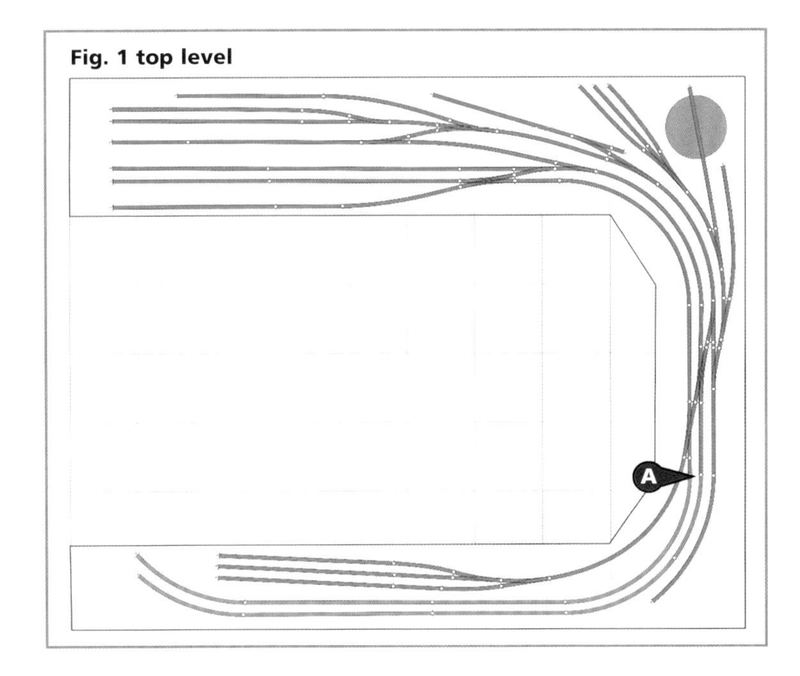

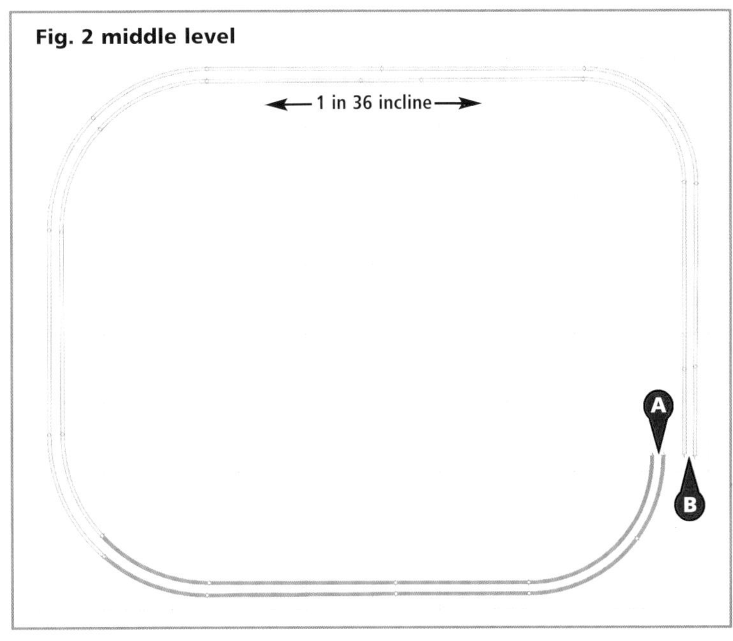

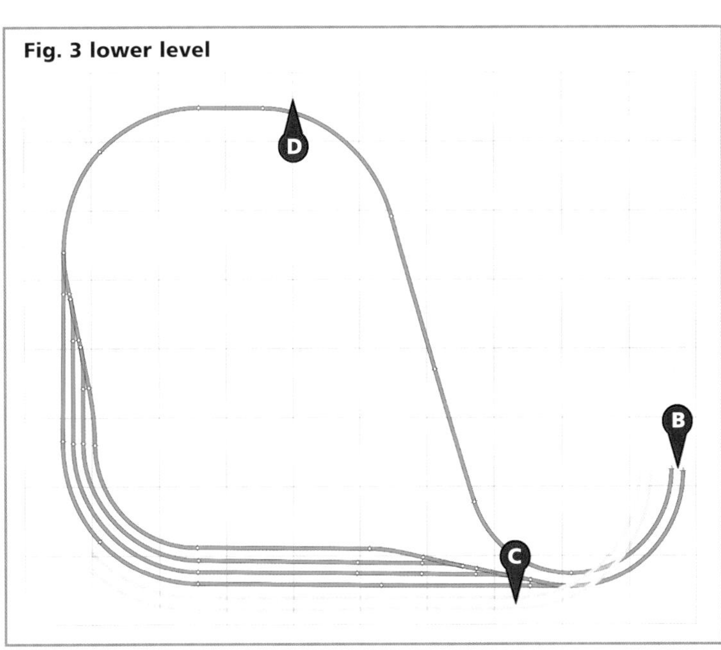

Robertstown, a multi-level OO gauge layout built by Owen Edis in his attic. Inclined tracks took the trains to several levels, some of which had storage loops directly below the scenic boards. Other hidden storage and return loops were located within the roof space – in the eaves – creating a complex but manageable set of levels. The layout was fully featured in the March 2015 issue of RAILWAY MODELLER.

Hannem Central

Plan 46 is a three-level concept devised by Graham Jowett-Ive and an arrangement which he used several times to create his *Hannem* layouts over several decades. In essence it takes Plan 45 a step further and includes a middle level on which a continuous run section is constructed. The isometric plan shows this to full effect. A train can leave the high level terminus and drop down to the middle level where, with the points set appropriately, it can be left to circulate for as long as desired. Then, resetting the points, the train can be directed to the lower level storage loops to await its eventual call to return back up to the inclines to the terminus. There is also a large locomotive depot and ample goods facilities for shunting activities. Truly a plan with end-to-end running, continuous running and shunting facilities all squeezed into a space (for OO gauge) of 14' x 8'.

Taking this plan as a starting point, the arrangement can be utilised in larger spaces to increase the visible continuous run and possibly include another through station. All in all plenty of scope for those with plenty of space.

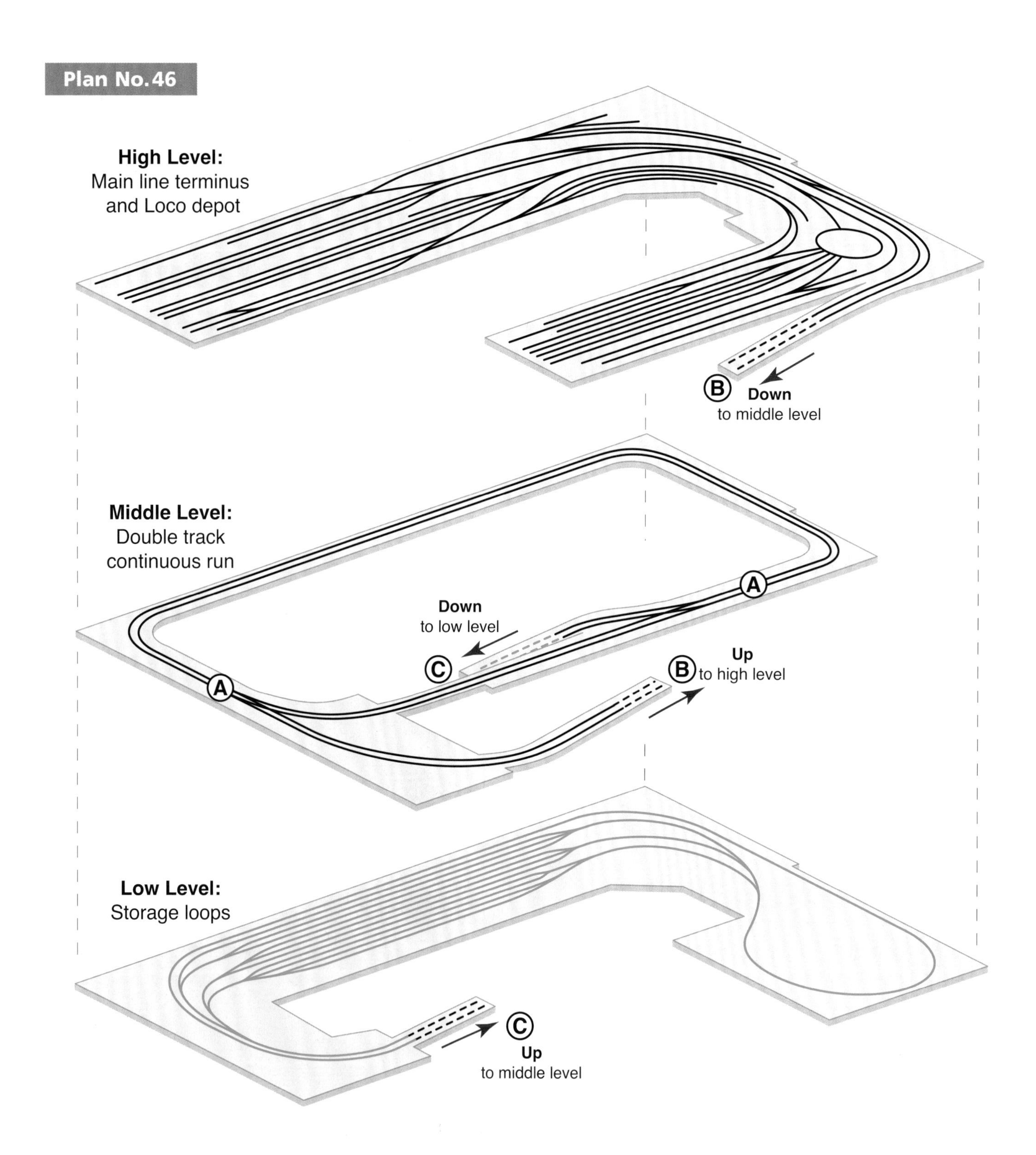

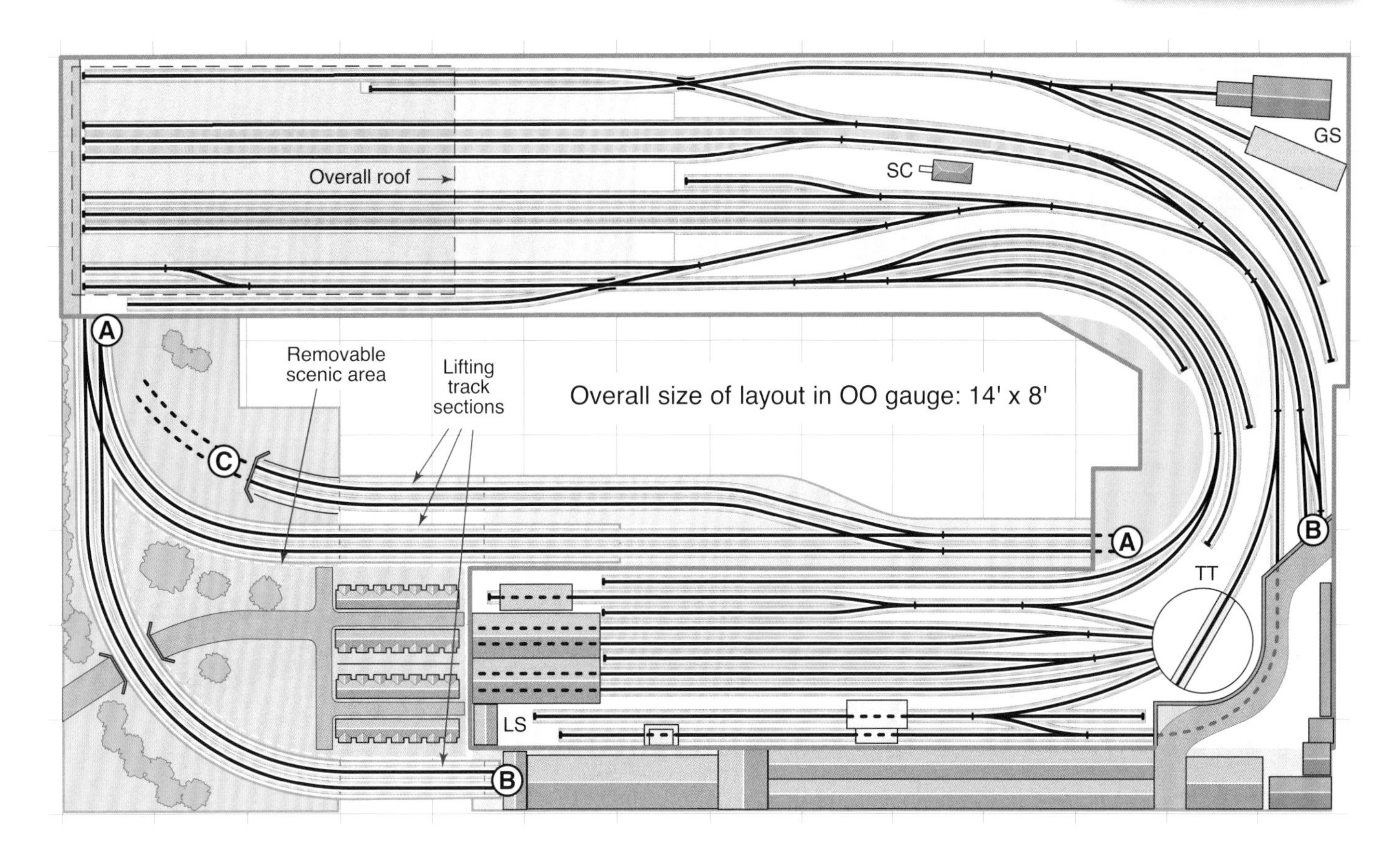

Below
This view across to the station throat on *Hannem Central* allows the three levels to be seen. The MPD covers the gradient from top to middle level – on which the King Arthur is running – and the fiddle yard can be seen below the terminus itself. Compare this view with that on page 39, of the same layout.

Chapter 7

Fold-away plans

Layouts that are displayed at all the exhibitions across the length and breadth of Britain – and there's one somewhere almost every weekend – are nearly all of the fold-away type, all designed to be split into manageable modules for ease of getting to and from the show venues. There are literally dozens and dozens of ways layouts can be made portable, with all sorts of well-tried designs, as well as some which are pretty unique. There are stacking systems for baseboards to travel on top of each other; crating systems which hold baseboards face to face to protect the delicate contents; even coffin-shaped lids to keep everything off. And then there are the supports; fold-up trestles with longitudinal beams; fold-down integral leg assemblies; plug-in standard leg modules; the list is almost endless as are the many ways of wiring such boards, all of which is beyond the scope of this book.

In this chapter we can't hope to cover all the methods and ideas, so we shall concentrate on just two. Firstly an idea that has been around since the early days of model railways – hinged boards. Essentially two, possibly three, of the boards are hinged so that they fold up concertina-like into a stack. A celebrated one dating from the 1950s was Revd. Peter Denny's original *Leighton Buzzard (Linslade)* – a simple two-board design with central back-flap hinges mounted on short vertical stubs – where the buildings on the layout were carefully positioned so that they didn't clash with each other when the layout was folded. Many modellers have used this concept and Gavin Thrum's plan *Great Moor Street* on page 21 took this a stage further linking three hinged boards which folded up into a crate. In this case the vertical stubs on which the hinges were mounted were disguised with a removable overbridge as shown. Other removable scenic structures, such as a building shell, or a hollow piece of scenery work just as well. The height of the vertical stubs needs to be such that sufficient space remains between the boards for buildings etc; higher structures and tall trees may need to be made remov-

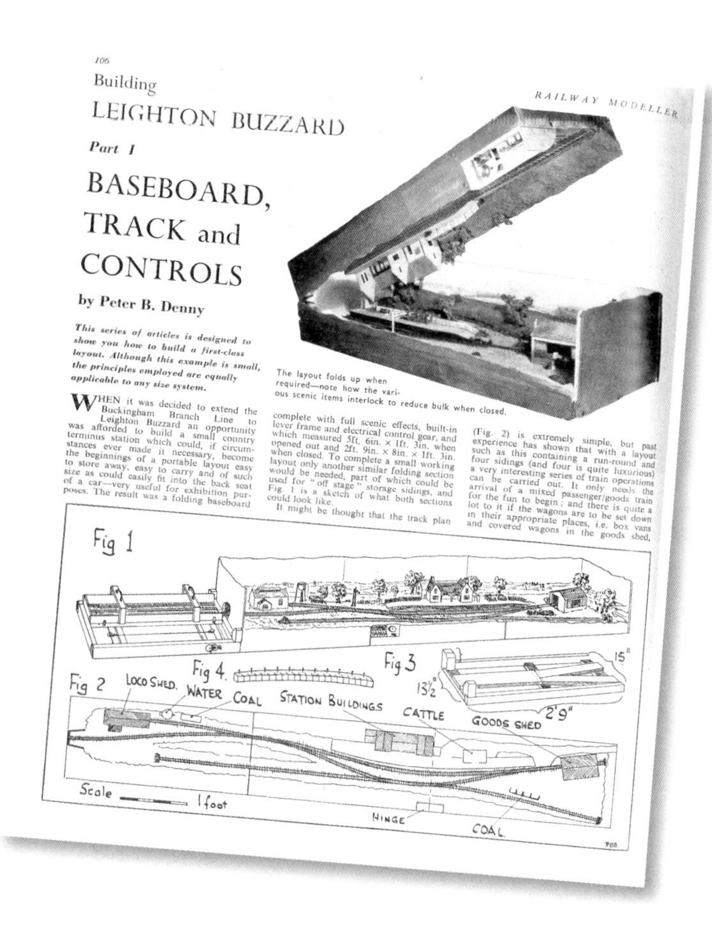

106

RAILWAY MODELLER

Building

LEIGHTON BUZZARD

Part I

BASEBOARD, TRACK and CONTROLS

by Peter B. Denny

This series of articles is designed to show you how to build a first-class layout. Although this example is small, the principles employed are equally applicable to any size system.

The layout folds up when required—note how the various scenic items interlock to reduce bulk when closed.

WHEN it was decided to extend the Buckingham Branch Line to Leighton Buzzard an opportunity was afforded to build a small country terminus station which could, if circumstances ever made it necessary, become the beginnings of a portable layout easy to store away, easy to carry and of such size as could easily fit into the back seat of a car—very useful for exhibition purposes. The result was a folding baseboard complete with full scenic effects, built-in lever frame and electrical control gear, and which measured 5ft. 6in. × 1ft. 3in. when opened out and 2ft. 9in. × 8in. × 1ft. 3in. when closed. To complete a small working layout only another similar folding section would be needed, part of which could be used for "off stage" storage sidings, and Fig. 1 is a sketch of what both sections could look like.

It might be thought that the track plan (Fig. 2) is extremely simple, but past experience has shown that with a layout such as this containing a run-round and four sidings (and four is quite luxurious) a very interesting series of train operations can be carried out. It only needs the arrival of a mixed passenger/goods train for the fun to begin; and there is quite a lot to it if the wagons are to be set down in their appropriate places, i.e. box vans and covered wagons in the goods shed,

Above
Hidden by a removable structure, the hinges on one side of the join are revealed; the other pair was masked from view by the station building.

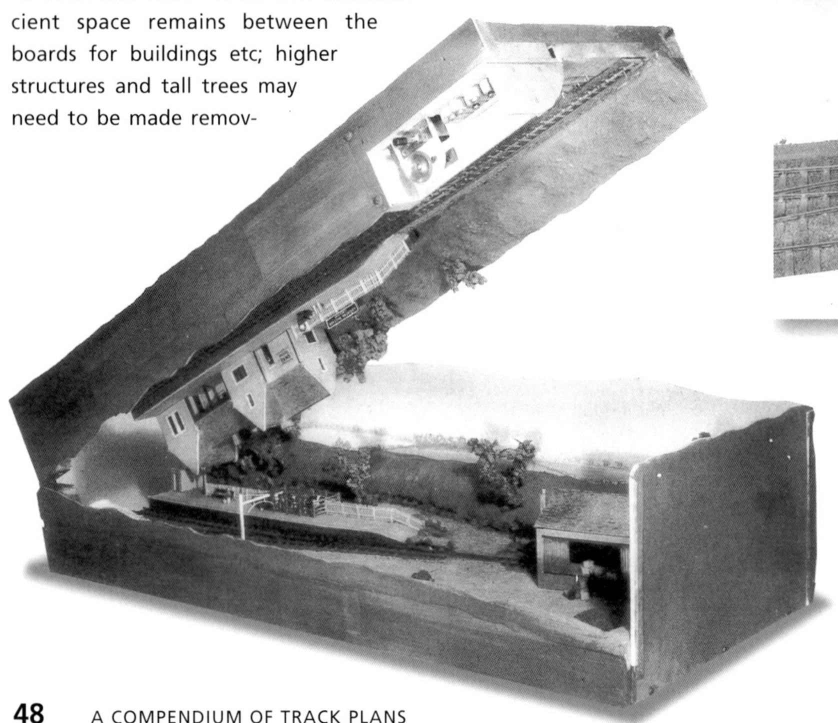

Left
Leighton Buzzard (Linslade) being folded up. The positions of the buildings and scenery needed to be taken note of when designing the layout, so that they could interlock to keep its folded depth to a minimum. *Photographs by Ron Doyle*

able. An end support will also be required at the open end, this need be nothing more than a board which can be bolted on.

Folding baseboards tend to be ideal for long, thin end-to-end layouts, though several such folding modules could be constructed and built into a full continuous run format if you have the inclination. An alternative way is to make the baseboard sections in modular sizes so that they can be stacked or crated together. We examine this alternative fold-away format with our two final plans.

As mentioned in the introduction, garages, cellars, spare rooms and the like, are usually taken over as temporary locations for this type of layout, but lounges and living rooms have been commandeered from time to time – even the illustrious Peter Denny built the first incarnation of his *Buckingham Branch Line* in the lounge of his London flat: but that's not everyone's cup of tea is it?

Above and right
Both sets of hinges are covered by removable road bridges – note the rebates for the hinges' knuckles themselves – and the bus goes along for the ride too!

Above
The arrangement of the three baseboards on *Great Moor Street* are best appreciated by studying the under-construction photo (top), from which it is clear that only the middle section is inverted for storage.

Below
In its operational state, an ex-LNWR Large Jumbo 2-4-0 prepares to depart the station. Period advertisements set an excellent sense of period.
Photographs on this page by Gavin Thrum

Plan No. 47

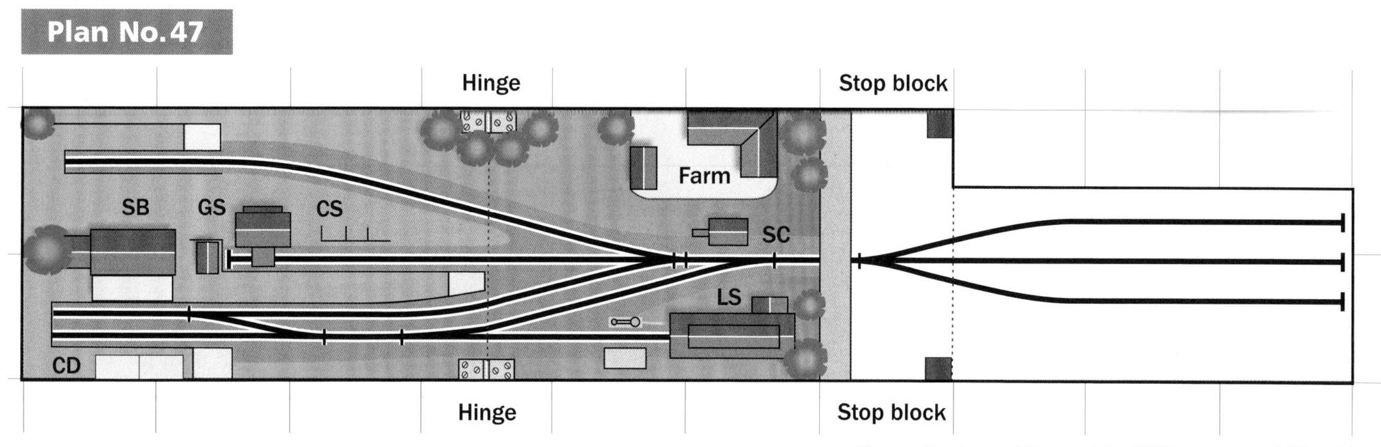

Overall size of layout in OO gauge: 10' x 2'

Woldway

Excuse the take on fold-away for the title of this plan! We imagine a rural hamlet served by a small branch line station with attendant goods facilities. The plan utilises two three-way points as space saving devices in both the scenic section and the fiddle yard. The two main boards are designed as the fold-together ones, with the hinges positioned on raised blocks as shown; these can be disguised by trees or shrubs. The fiddle yard board is shown as a smaller bolt-on module, to keep the overall length under 10' in OO gauge. This could however be a third board to the same length and width as the two main boards (ie 3'6"), the extra 6" would enable the hidden sidings to be extended a little to allow for slightly longer train lengths.

Plan No. 48

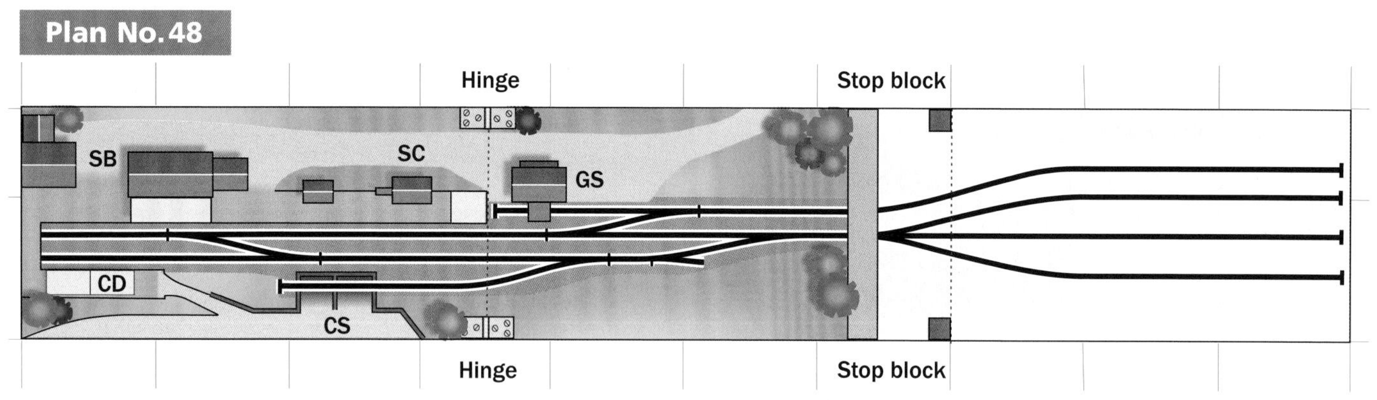

Overall size of layout in OO gauge: 10' x 1' 6"

Woldway Lane

An alternative version of the above idea but using a narrower baseboard – this time all three are just 20" wide in OO gauge. The headshunt for the goods shed siding is allowed to run through into the fiddle yard allowing us to suppose that a loco shed or other freight siding is located off scene. When folded the goods shed and station master's house may need to be removable as clearances will be tight. Once again a space-saving three-way point is used to help keep maximum length around 10'. Folding designs such as these are also easily translated for use in other scales. In N gauge either of these plans would fold up very small. For O gauge note that the baseboards will be proportionally larger and heavier.

Below
A typical country goods yard with NER style coal drops on *Brough*, as modelled by members of Birtley Model Engineers.

Plan No. 49

Mereton

We now turn our attention to ideas using modular stackable baseboards. This plan is based on a similar small layout built in OO gauge by Stuart Robinson some years ago which he called *Mere*. *Mereton* uses three baseboards; two of which are just 1' x 4' long, with the third being 2' x 4' such that they will either stack, or crate together. It is yet another familiar branch line terminus scheme, but this time the run-round loop is not placed adjacent to the platform, as with convention. It is positioned as part of the curved section of track, allowing some goods facilities to be included on the narrow station board. The overall area occupied by the fully erected layout is just 6' x 4' in OO gauge and in order for it to be viable, the curved points in the loop are from the Peco Setrack range. Note that pointwork is just clear of the baseboard joints, making both construction and alignment across the gap relatively straightforward.

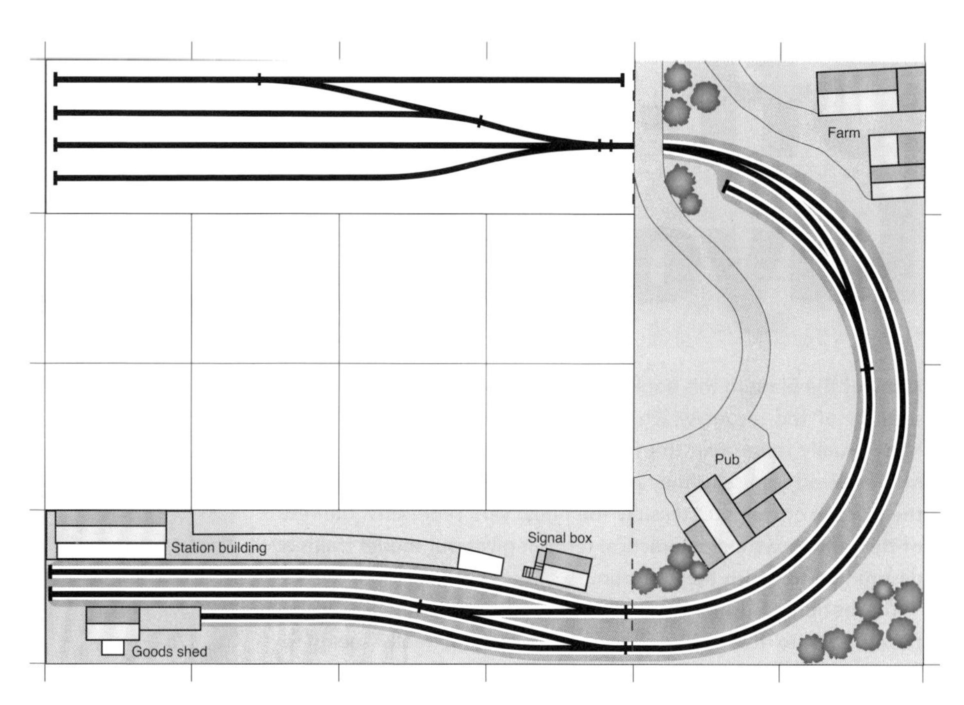

Overall size of layout in OO gauge: 6' x 4'

Plan No. 50

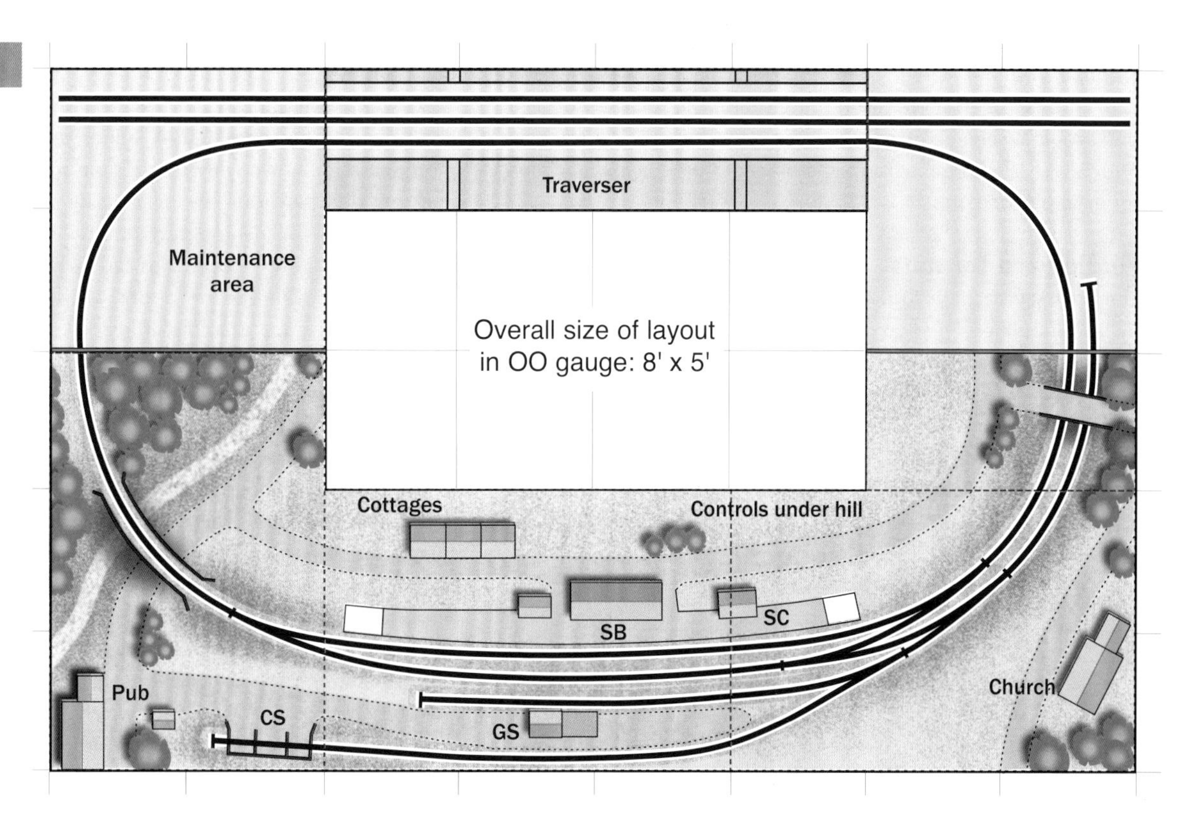

This plan uses modular sized boards for a continuous run theme. There are four 2' x 3' main boards, one 4' x 1' board with traverser, and one 2' x 2' board that when assembled occupy an area of only 8' x 5' (2.438m x 1.525m): a size that should fit in most spare bedrooms. For storage, the main boards crate together face-to-face using end spacers to form two boxes. The traverser lifts off and the 4' x 1' board splits, or folds, to crate up with the 2' x 2' board, forming a third storage box.

When erected, the boards are joined by bolts and to support the whole layout, folding gate leg units, 2' x 2', one in each outer corner and smaller ones, 1' x 1' on each inside corner, could be used. In OO the plan is drawn for use with flexible track and Peco curved points, creating sweeping compound curves within the scenic section. Behind the scenes, the radius is reduced to 18". Controls can be built into the hillside as shown, with wiring connected between boards via multi-way plugs and sockets.

Chapter 8

Off-stage layout sections

Many of the plans in this book either include, or refer to, off-stage sections of the layout which are colloquially called fiddle yards. Most usually these take the form of sections of layout which are not rendered scenically, they are just bare baseboards and track for the storage of trains. Ostensibly the fiddle yard represents the rest of the railway system: in practical terms it gives our model trains a destination to which they can run.

The notion of using a fiddle yard as off-scene storage can be traced back to the 1920s, although the concept really seems to have taken off in the 1950s and is now one of those standard practices firmly embedded in the culture of model railways.

Fiddle yards come in many shapes, sizes and degrees of engineering complexity, though when reduced to the basics, they come in two configurations; single or double ended. Single ended yards are used with end-to-end layouts; one yard with a terminus layout, two yards (one at either end) on a through station layout, as seen for example, with the plans in chapter 4. Double ended yards are used with continuous run layouts and often form the rear half or so of the layout, as seen on plans in chapter 5, but may also be arranged on a lower level baseboard for permanent home layouts as seen, for example, on page 44.

Fiddle yard formats

There are several basic formats of fiddle yard which are widely used by layout builders. First up is the Ladder Yard. This is probably the easiest fiddle yard to construct, and the most railway-like in its operation. It is a set of loops or dead end sidings fed from a fan or fans of points.

It holds no fresh modelling challenges since the construction of one requires the same skills necessary for laying the track and

Above
A ladder fiddleyard on Dean Knights' OO loft layout *Pen-Hill.*

points on the scenic sections of the layout. In some ways it is quicker, as scenic ballasting is not required and any point motors used don't need to be concealed. A ladder yard does however require more space for a given amount of train storage than the other formats of fiddle yard that we will consider shortly. This is due to the space required for the approach pointwork, although the inclusion of 3-way points and double slips can help.

A distinct advantage of ladder yards constructed as one-way return loops (as, for example, in plans 45 and 46) is that they can be automated by various electronic means when point motors are employed, particularly useful for DCC devotees considering a means of computer control. Furthermore such yards mean that trains don't have to be handled at any point during their traverse of the yard, unless of course, you wish to remarshall the vehicles.

So ladder yards are straightforward to build, but are a little space hungry and can be cumbersome if used on a fold-away or portable layout. Consequently modellers have developed a few space saving dodges for the hidden siding section which involve the physical movement of the hidden sidings themselves. The principles behind their operation and construction are broadly similar in that each method employs a moving deck which is used to align the hidden tracks with the inlet/exit tracks in turn, thereby saving the entire length of any approach pointwork that would otherwise be installed.

The various designs of moving deck mechanisms differ slightly in their application and flexibility so we shall examine each one in turn as follows.

Left
An interesting combination of fiddle yard loops and dead-end storage sidings on Ian Stoate's N gauge *Walcot Yard* exhibition layout.

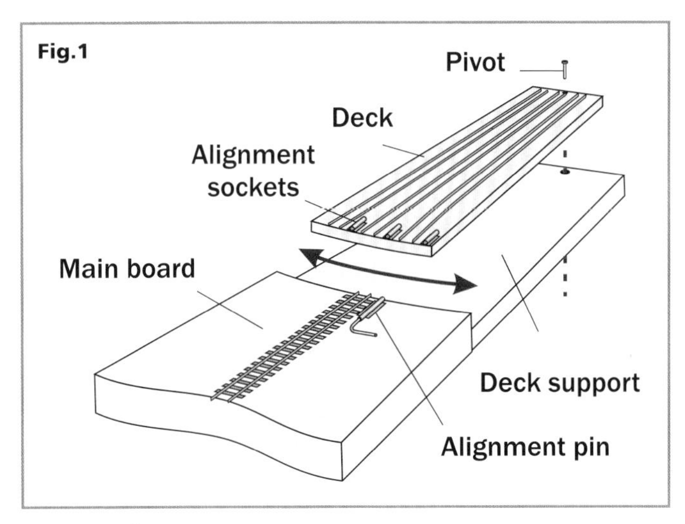

The sector plate arrangement on Neil Rushby's *Abergwynant* 4mm scale layout.

Sector plates

These are the simplest of the moving deck mechanisms. Many of the smaller schemes in this book make use of a sector plate, such as plans 4, 5, 8 and 10. It need be no more than a pivoting deck of thin timber, such that it can be laid on the main baseboard surface. The end of the sector plate that links to the entry/exit track(s) on the rest of the layout is cut in an arc which has its centre at the pivot point, as shown in Fig. 1. Most sheet timber used for baseboard surfaces; chipboard, MDF, plywood etc, can be used for the moving deck and the most important consideration is ensuring that there is an absolutely smooth and level transition of track between the two parts.

A method of aligning the tracks accurately is desirable and many enthusiasts use sliding brass barrel bolts to accomplish this as they can also be used for an automatic electrical connection to the corresponding siding – see Fig. 2. If using DCC of course, each siding can be permanently live, otherwise the bolt thus acts as both an alignment dowel and a 'section switch' at the same time.

A sector plate is generally best suited to a single track exit/entry yard in tight spaces. The ends of all the tracks must be absolutely perpendicular to the arc of the joint, so twin track sector exit/entry plates need more lateral space as the tracks need to be splayed out to fit with the geometry.

Traversers

This mechanism is essentially a deck which slides back and forth, like a drawer, so as to link in with any number of exit/entry tracks. All tracks have to be equally spaced, and the traverser can be single or double ended, making it useful for continuous run plans, such as plan 13 or plan 50, for example.

Construction of traversers can be similar to that used for sector plates, though some modellers use drawer slides to minimise friction when sliding as in Fig. 3. Alignment and electrical connections can again be provided by sliding metal barrel bolts. If using a traverser on a home layout that is to be fixed to the wall, take care to position the entry/exit tracks sufficiently clear of the back wall so that the traverser can travel to its full design span both forwards and backwards.

Fig. 2

Main baseboard
Deck support
Deck
Section switches
To controller

Making electrical connections to a sector plate using the hard-wired method. Each siding is isolated by a separate section switch, though if using DCC they can be eliminated

Alignment pin
Alignment socket on each sector plate track

Metal barrel bolts, as used on cupboard doors, can be used to both align the tracks and act as the isolating switches

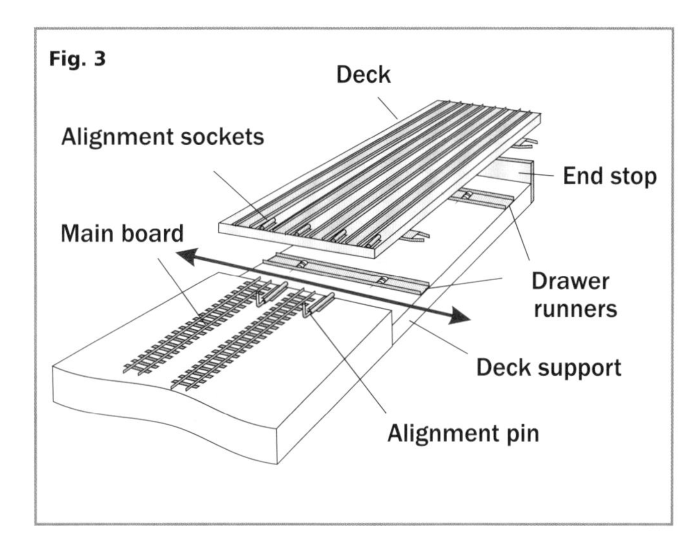

Below
Frecclesham, the 7mm scale Southern Region layout of Newport Model Railway Society uses a traverser.

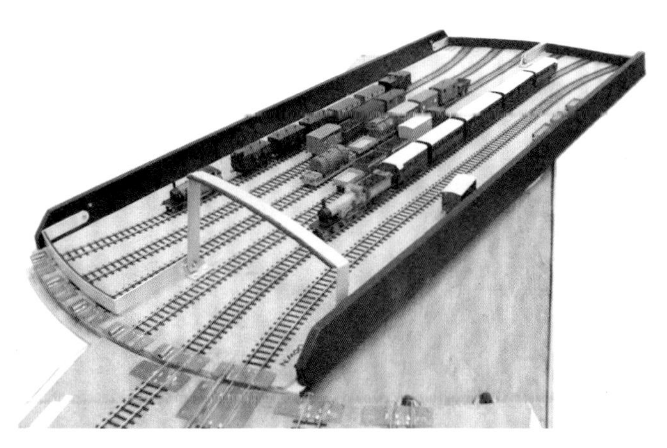

Above
A complete train turntable as used on *Burntisland*, the award winning layout built by the East of Scotland 4mm Group of the Scalefour Society.

Train turntables

A train turntable is essentially a traverser which instead of moving to and fro, rotates through a full 180°. In some ways it is essentially just a double-ended version of a sector plate with the pivot in the centre. But there are perhaps a few factors worth bearing in mind.

- the mating faces of the turntable and adjacent board must be perfectly circular – otherwise the table might jam when turned fully.
- all entry/exit tracks must cross the join perpendicular to the circumference of the turntable, so as with sector plates, parallel entry/exit tracks must similarly be splayed outward.
- you will have to arrange the electrical feeds through the bolt and socket method, as a hard wired umbilical cord won't allow a 180° rotation – at least not more than once!

Side walls to the deck are a good idea to protect the stock as it rotates out from the footprint of the underlying baseboard, and some form of end gate to prevent loose stock rolling off the ends whilst turning is advisable too as shown in the photo of the train turntable on the award-winning *Burntisland* historical layout.

Train turntables are very useful for sequence operations and all but eliminate any stock handling off-scene, save perhaps for the occasional exchange of locomotives. One significant disadvantage of a train turntable is that it cannot be used up against a wall; it

Above
Peter Denny's train turntable on *Buckingham* photographed c.1960. This unit was drawn back away from the join with the layout prior to turning.
Photograph by Ronald Doyle

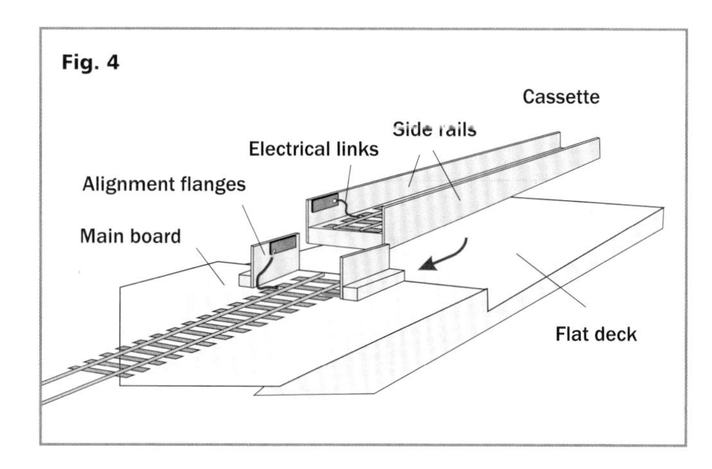

must be located somewhere where it can be allowed to rotate fully, useful mostly therefore on freestanding layout sections in the centre of a room. The idea is not new, the late Revd. Peter Denny used a similar configuration over 50 years ago on his famous *Buckingham Branch Line* layout, as seen in the accompanying photograph. His yard slid backwards away from the join, which was square, and rotated fully before being pushed forward again to reconnect with the entry/exit tracks.

Cassette storage

A train storage cassette is a length of track on an independent rigid base which plugs or clips onto the end of the fixed track on the main layout at the point where it exits from the scenic section as in Fig. 4. The cassette, complete with train, is then unplugged and either stored aside, or turned around and plugged back in place so the same train can be returned immediately. If stored aside, another cassette containing a different train can be plugged in ready for use. To enable all this to work, the fiddle yard baseboard is usually made as a flat deck to support the cassettes and allow them to be shuffled as required. You can have as many cassettes as you wish, increasing the storage facility of the fiddle yard without having to lay any more points or make the boards wider. The cassettes can be designed to stack on top of each other and allow storage elsewhere; on shelves, or on racking above the layout, or even in portable stock boxes designed to take loaded units. Furthermore, as points are not needed, there is a cost saving, and track alignment is far easier to accomplish than with sector plates or traversers, as only one pair of track ends has to be matched up.

As with train turntables, side walls and end gates are a good idea to counter the risk of stock rolling off whilst being moved. Both rails must align accurately to avoid derailments and the track current needs to be connected. Relying on rail joiners alone is not a good idea as they will undoubtably wear loose. Two alternative suggestions are shown in Fig. 5.

The only main disadvantage is that there is a maximum practical length of cassette, probably about 5' long, as anything longer will be unwieldy to manoeuvre and difficult to build rigid along its length. Maximum train length will thus be limited to relatively short trains in OO – four coaches plus loco.

A popular version of the cassette concept utilises the Peco Loco Lift, a useful kit which embodies the features of a short cassette with its base designed to sit directly on the rail top and simultaneously align the rails and make electrical contact. It comes in easy to assemble flat pack form and is principally intended as an easy way to lift locos off the track without causing damage or getting fingerprints all over the paintwork. It can only be used on straight OO gauge track, but only a short length needs overlapping for align-

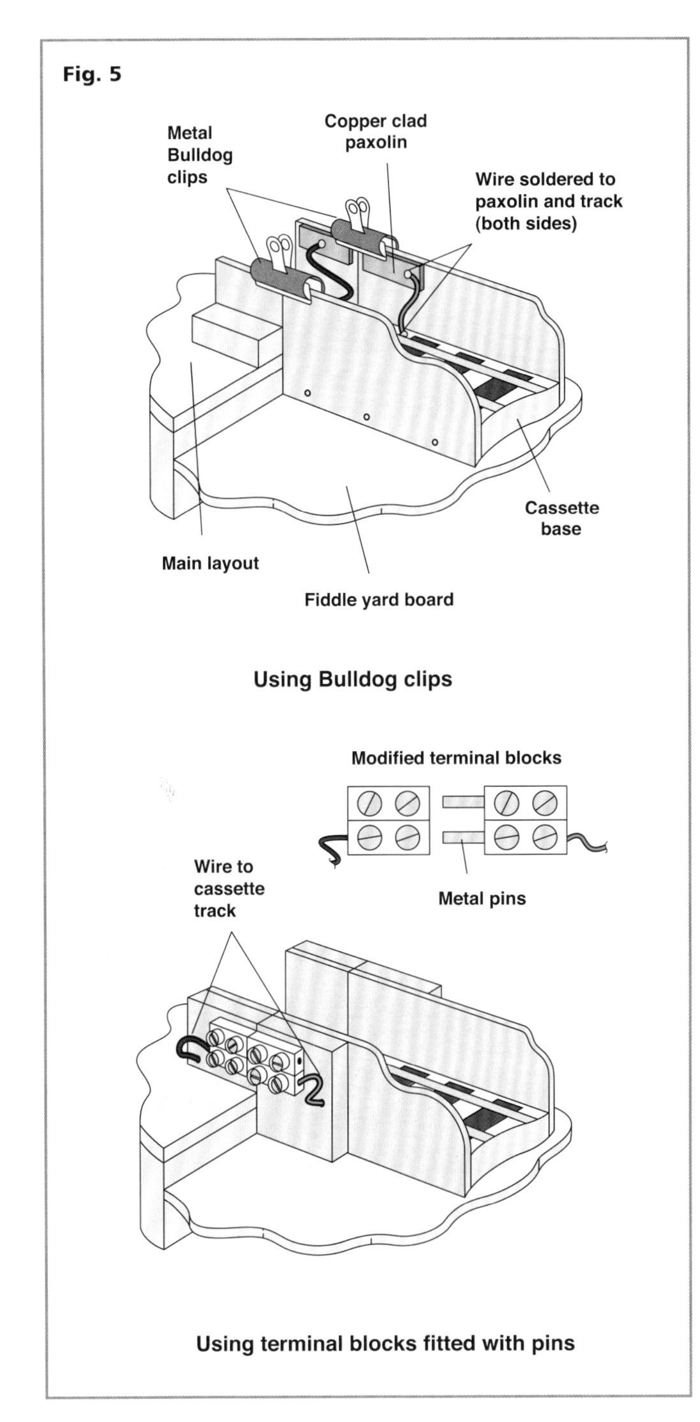

Above
The Loco Lift in use as a cassette on Richard Peake's *Castle Wharf Yard*. His plan for this compact layout appears on page 11.

ment and electrical contact. Richard Peake's plan, No.9, utilised a Peco Loco Lift in this way.

What several modellers have done is to combine three or four Loco Lifts into a long cassette by replacing the soft plastic sides with ¼" timber battens of appropriate length and fitting the lifting handles at each end only. An example of this adaptation is shown in the photograph of Stephen Shepherd's *Kimpton* layout. Again the beauty of this assembly is automatic track alignment and electrical contact without any additional fittings.

The choice is yours

Nearly all the plans in this book include some sort of off-stage train storage, and in most cases, any one of the various formats of fiddle yard described here can be adopted for use. There is no right or wrong choice of a fiddle yard, other than being aware that it must fit and function in the space you have available, and if locating underneath a scenic board it is useful to design in as much access space as possible.

Above
The Peco Loco Lift doubles up as a short cassette which can also be used for short rakes of wagons.

Stephen Shepherd linked three Loco Lift kits together to provide this 3' cassette as used on his L-shaped *Kimpton* OO gauge layout.

SUBSCRIBE

AND GET THE VERY BEST IN

PLUS!

WHILST YOU SUBSCRIBE TO RAILWAY MODELLER OR CONTINENTAL MODELLER YOU WILL HAVE

FREE MONTHLY ACCESS

TO THE *DIGITAL EDITION OF THAT MAGAZINE AT NO EXTRA CHARGE.

*Available for PC, Mac, Smartphone or Tablet. **iOS** and **Android OS** devices supported *(see website for details).*

TODAY! RAILWAY MODELLING

Great Britain's No.1 model railway magazines

every month!

CONTINENTAL MODELLER

FEATURING RAILWAYS FROM AROUND THE WORLD EACH MONTH

Drei Spurenhof
German HO/HOe/HOf

Also in this issue...

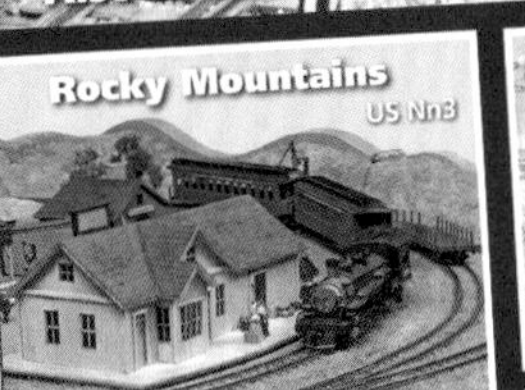

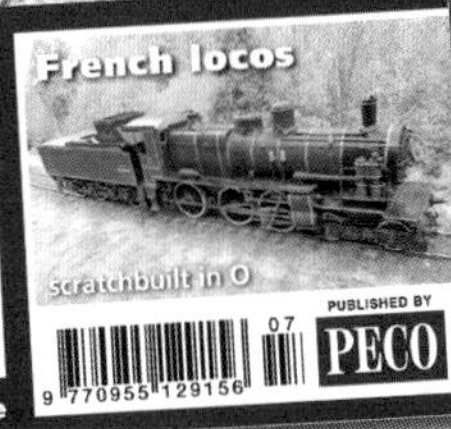

Latest Reviews ... and much more

PUBLISHED BY PECO

Digital editions include fully searchable back issues starting from Jan 2011.

You can take up a subscription to RAILWAY MODELLER & CONTINENTAL MODELLER by post, by telephone, or online.

It's easy, so subscribe today!

Peco Publications & Publicity,
Beer, Devon EX12 3NA, England
Tel: 01297 626203
www.pecopublications.co.uk

Chapter 9

Creating your own plans

For anyone wanting to have a go at developing a model railway layout plan of their own, we are including in this final chapter some advice, hints and tips about the planning process. The key issues to consider are; time, budget, where you will house the layout, and what you want to achieve with it. Building a model railway can often take many years, so making the right choices on these will ensure long-lasting enjoyment and fulfilment.

Making a start

When you have thought about what you want to achieve with your layout, you can begin the process of generating a track plan which will include the locations of buildings, platforms, bridges, hidden sidings, etc. This is a creative process and can be both challenging and fun, and usually costs very little money. The first thing you need to determine is the dimensions of the space available for the layout, or if building a portable one, the dimensions that it is to occupy when fully erected. This gives you the template or boundary within which your design must fit. With that crucial factor determined, you can then proceed with track planning.

These days there are several computer software packages that can help you develop a full plan. One popular package is AnyRail™ which is compatible with Windows PC machines and can be purchased as a download from the internet.

Right
Peco Design Engineer David Malton tries out the AnyRail™ track planning software.

Fig. 1: **Suggested Minimum Planning Dimensions – inches** (mm)
For standard gauge railways in popular scales

Scale/Gauge	N	OO	Gauge O	Gauge 1
Point length (med. radius)	5½ (140)	8½ (216)	16 (406)	24 (610)
Crossover (long)	11½ (292)	18 (457)	34 (866)	42 (1067)
Minimum track centres	1 (25)	2 (50)	3½ (90)	4⅓ (110)
Minimum radius curves	9 (229)	18 (457)	48 (1220)	72 (1829)
Minimum platform width	1¼ (32)	2½ (64)	4¾ (120)	6 (152)
Min. overhead clearance	1½ (38)	3 (75)	6 (152)	9 (229)
Average coach (64')	5½ (140)	10½ (267)	18 (457)	26 (660)
Typical wagon (10' wb.)	2 (50)	3½ (90)	6¼ (158)	9 (228)

Minimum length of loco release = length of loco over buffers + 10%
Suggested minimum length of headshunt = longest loco + three longest wagons

These dimensions are nominal and meant as a guide for use when sketching out ideas.
Always check out your plans with trials using paper point templates.

Fig. 2: **The Basic Elements of Track Formations**

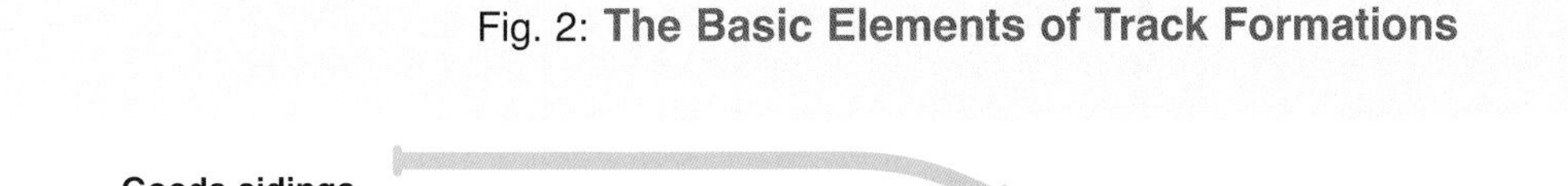
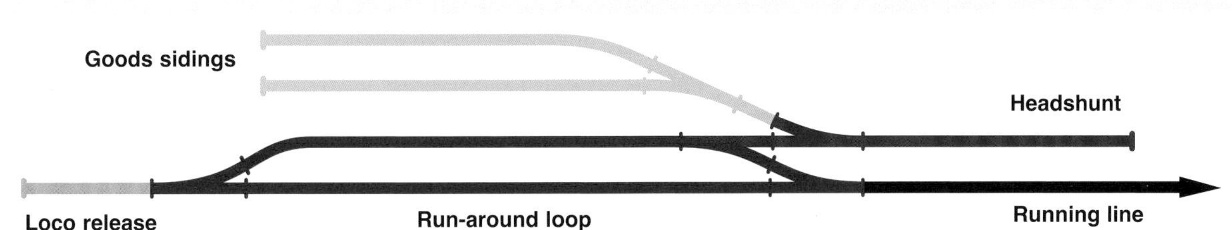

Run-around loop
This allows a locomotive to uncouple from its train and run around to the other end usually in order to pull it back in the opposite direction. It must be long enough to hold the longest trains you wish to run.

Loco release
An essential part of a run around loop. The length of the loco release track will determine the largest loco you can operate on your layout.

Headshunt
In order to place wagons in the goods sidings the loco will pull the train into the headshunt and then reverse to push them into the sidings. The length of the headshunt will dictate how long a train can be shunted in one operation.

Sidings
Wagons must always be propelled into these areas otherwise the loco will be trapped by the wagons. Athough sidings can also be loops, with loco access from either end.

It is easy to use and includes component templates for all brands of proprietary track, including Peco Streamline and Setrack in all the scales and gauges. Other dedicated track planning packages available via the internet include, XtrackCad, WinRail, and Templot. Although computer aided design in this way can be useful, many modellers still start with some pencil sketches of their ideas, perhaps using the software at a later stage in the process as a means of checking the viability of the plan and collating a list of components.

Critical dimensions

There is certainly no need for elaborate computer software, a pencil and a soft rubber is really all you need to try out your ideas on paper first. Creating a track plan can be split into three distinct stages; initial sketches, a scale drawing, and practical checks.

When making the initial sketches, you will need to ensure that critical dimensions of items such as points and crossovers, minimum track centres, etc, are adhered to. Otherwise you end with a plan that just isn't workable in practice because you've squeezed in far too much. As a guide to help anyone considering drawing up their own scheme we have included the accompanying table (Fig. 1) of suggested minimum planning dimensions. They are given in both inches and millimetres.

Choosing a suitable scale for your sketches is important. Those using imperial measurements might use, for convenience, one inch to one foot. If you are working in metric you could work at 1:10 or 1:25; graph paper is useful as it is divided into 10 x 10 squares. As you are aiming for a layout plan that includes all the elements in your list, it will be a trial and error process and it usually takes several sketches, each slightly different, until you arrive at something with which you are happy.

Trackwork elements

If you look at other layouts in magazines or at exhibitions, or at published plans in books like these, and even the prototype railway, in almost all of them you will see that the formations are made up from various common trackwork elements. These include run-around loops, headshunts and goods sidings. Knowing the effect each element has on the running of trains will help you identify how you should use them in the layout. Fig. 2 shows the most common elements and includes explanations of their purpose.

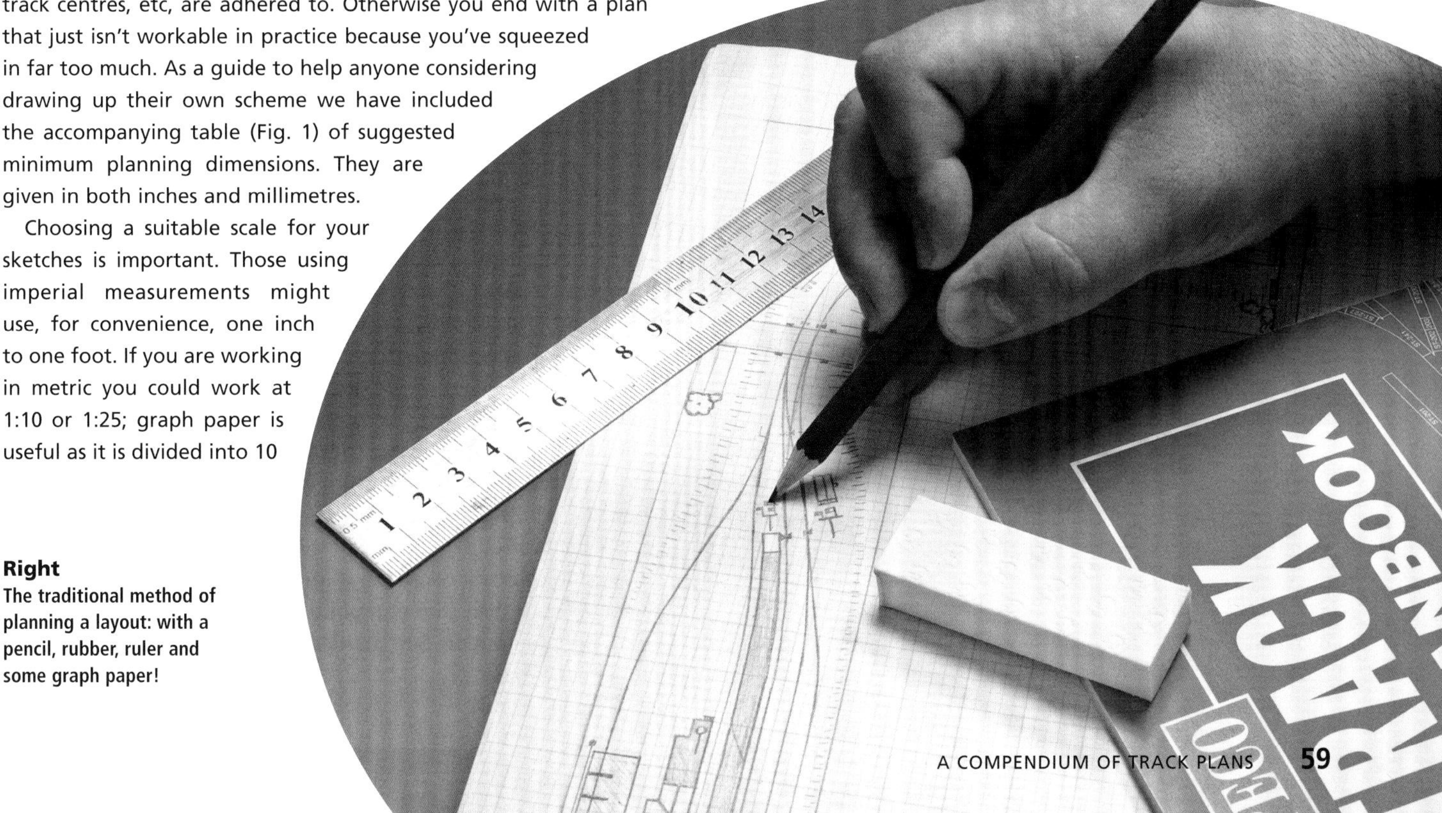

Right
The traditional method of planning a layout: with a pencil, rubber, ruler and some graph paper!

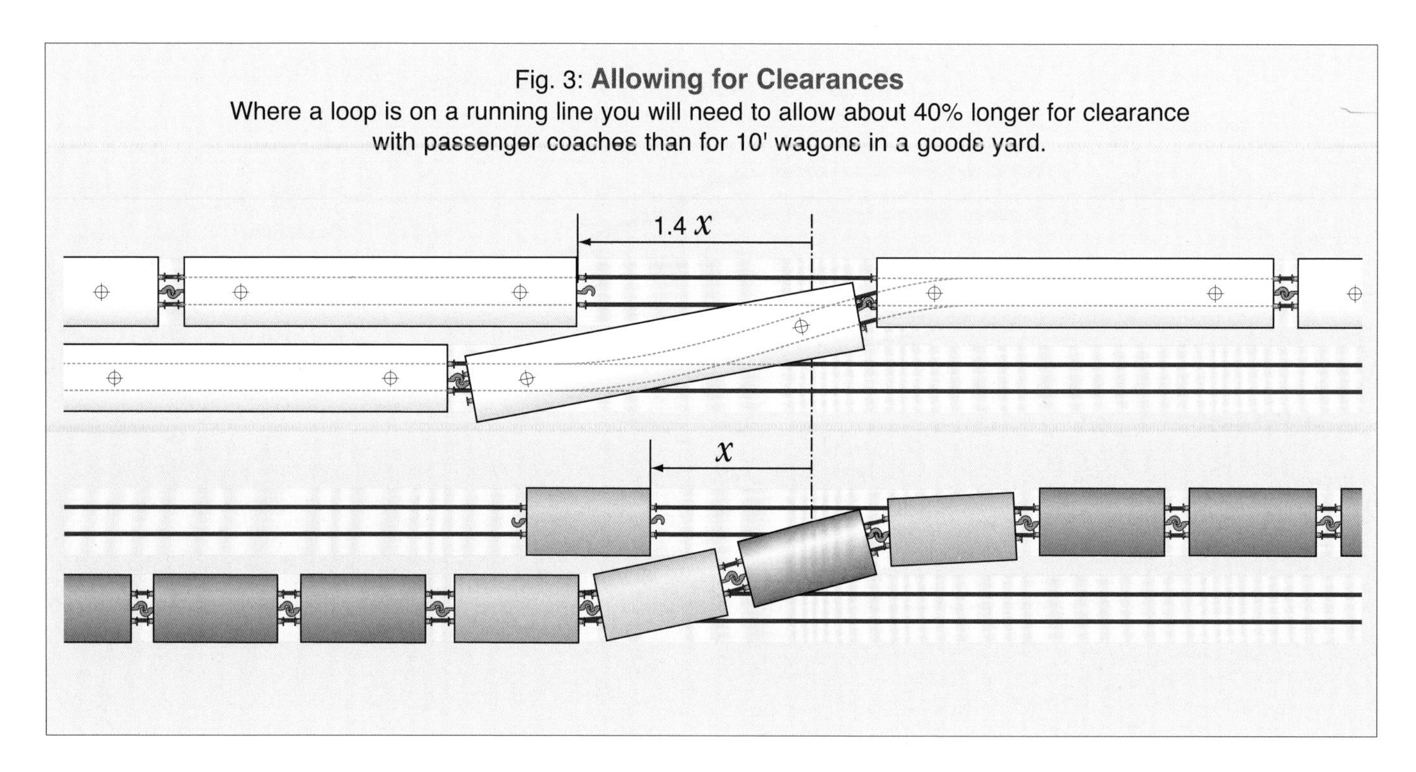

Fig. 3: **Allowing for Clearances**
Where a loop is on a running line you will need to allow about 40% longer for clearance with passenger coaches than for 10' wagons in a goods yard.

The most important element is usually a run-around loop, and almost every layout should have one especially if you are modelling a terminus station in the steam period. The critical feature of a run-around loop is that it dictates the maximum length of train you can operate. The whole train must fit within the loop so that the locomotive can get to the other end of the train. To run a six-coach passenger train, the length of the loop must be six coaches long plus enough clearance at either end to stop the locomotive fouling the coaches as it passes them, see Fig. 3.

Often the size and position of this feature is the starting point from which the rest of the layout design evolves. Sketch that in and then work up from there, adding curves perhaps or some more points feeding goods sidings. If, as you progress, you realise that it just won't fit, then shorten your train length by one coach and start the sketching process again.

Eventually you will have a design that includes all or most of the requirements in your original idea. At this stage it is worthwhile to put it to one side for a day or two, and see if you are still satisfied with it when you come to look at it again. If not, start the process all over again and when all seems OK, you can then move onto the next stage.

Scale Plans

You can now translate your sketch into a full scale working plan. Many modellers like to do this as it helps to check the feasibility of their ideas, but it is not always essential and you can miss out this stage and move straight on to the practical checks section.

If you decide to prepare a scale plan you will not need much equipment, but good quality paper or card is preferable. Some French curves for drawing will be helpful, but you can use a pair of compasses, or even make your own scale curve templates out of stiff card. At this stage, use of one of the aforementioned computer design packages can help you prepare your scale plan if you have the equipment at your disposal.

Practical Checks

By now, you have identified the space in which you are going to build the layout, taken measurements and prepared either a viable sketch plan or an accurate scale plan. If you feel confident about your plans you can now start building the baseboards. However, it is a good idea to make some practical checks at this stage to verify the feasibility of your plan before you spend any money. It is also well worth going through this final stage of practical checks even if you are using a published plan and there are a number of ways to do this.

Paper Track Templates

For many years Peco has printed sheets of full-size templates for each of its ranges of Streamline and Setrack points and crossings. They can be cut out from the sheet for positioning or photocopied. You can use them either directly where the layout is going, or by pasting them onto some lining paper cut to the size of the baseboards. With lining paper you can draw in the plain track sections with a pencil. Using paper templates in this way is a reliable and inexpensive way of checking your plan. OO/HO templates can now be downloaded free as printable pdf files from the Peco website. www.peco-uk.com (Other scales will follow).

Full Size Trials

If, like many modellers, you already possess some items of pointwork, plain track lengths, etc, you can use these as full size 'templates', effectively mocking-up the track plan with actual components. It would be fair to say that this method, if used in conjunction with paper templates, is actually an acceptable substitute for the scale drawing stage: you can go straight from your initial sketch to a full-size trial.

Visualisation mock-ups

The above techniques enable the track configuration to be checked for accuracy. With visualisation mock-ups you can get an idea of how the whole scene will look. Essentially the proposed buildings are assembled quickly in card to the intended size and positioned alongside your trackwork mock-up or templates. Viewed from all sides you can then trim or reposition them until you are satisfied with the composition. Such mock-ups can be created at full size or to a smaller scale.